DOLLS, PUPPEDOLLS,™ AND TEDDY BEARS

DOLLS, PUPPEDOLLS, AND TEDDY BEARS

Estelle Ansley Worrell

VAN NOSTRAND REINHOLD COMPANY
New York Cincinnati Toronto London Melbourne

To Norman

**Who always says "Go ahead,
you can do it, I know you can."**

Printed in the United States of America
Designed by Loudan Enterprises
The black-and-white and color photographs are by Henry D. Widick.

Published in 1977 by Van Nostrand Reinhold Company
A division of Litton Educational Publishing, Inc.
135 West 50th Street, New York, N.Y. 10020

Van Nostrand Reinhold Limited
1410 Birchmount Road, Scarborough, Ontario M1P 2E7, Canada

Van Nostrand Reinhold Australia Pty. Limited
17 Queen Street, Mitcham, Victoria 3132, Australia

Van Nostrand Reinhold Company Limited
Molly Millars Lane, Wokingham, Berkshire, England

16 15 14 13 12 11 10 9 8 7 6 5 4 3 2

Library of Congress Cataloging in Publication Data

Worrell, Estelle Ansley, 1929–
    Dolls, puppedolls, and teddy bears.

    Includes index.
    1. Dollmaking. 2. Puppet making. 3. Teddy
bears. I. Title.
TT175.W67   745.59'22   77-7246
ISBN 0-442-29541-3

Contents

Introduction

For too many years cloth has been used merely to enhance other forms of dolls, rather than as an art form in its own right. Even when attempts were made to use cloth as the medium, the artists usually added another material for the doll's face rather than meet the design challenges within the medium. In Germany in 1912 Kathe Kruse started making her beautiful cloth dolls with metal reinforced faces. In Italy in 1921 the Lenci Doll Company was started. The felt, used for the dolls, was stiffened and machine pressed to manufacture the faces. Later the bodies were of pressed, stiffened cloth also.

I decided, therefore, to accept the limitations of cloth without being intimidated by them and to create dolls of beauty and purity. I also decided to make that medium, cloth, respond to me and to what I wanted of it! I truly feel that the art of the cloth doll has only begun to be explored.

The cloth doll is probably as old as cloth itself, having been found in Egyptian tombs. But the cloth doll, as we know it, is really an American phenomenon.

The cloth doll has always been quite common in America, so common in fact that it has been taken for granted. It was always the "everyday doll" or the bedtime doll, which was the one truly loved while the expensive, fragile, imported or hand-carved doll was the "Sunday" or "holiday" one to be brought out on special days for supervised play. The rag doll was worn out or literally "loved to pieces" while the Sunday doll was carefully preserved for succeeding generations.

There were patents for cloth dolls in America in the last part of the nineteenth century but the cloth doll and cloth toy animal really came into their own in the early twentieth century. An early form of "do your-own" dolls was the printed doll of 1900 in the U.S. and 1903 in London that could be cut out and sewn together at home. The Teddy bear and the Raggedy Ann doll were immensely popular. The Teddy bear was created in 1908–1910 and Raggedy Ann, in 1915–1918. The Teddy bear craze and the English *Winnie-the-Pooh* stories made the soft, cloth toy popular with boys as well as girls for the first time. Of the millions sold, many were for young boys. Nobody could call a boy a sissy for cuddling a bear, now could they? Raggedy Ann, popular at the end of the second decade, had a Raggedy Andy boy companion doll. Although "Andy" was still primarily a girl's toy there were young boys who were allowed to own him, too.

Today, boys are encouraged to play with dolls—masculine dolls mostly of the spy and military type but of the baby-doll type, too. Kindergartens and nursery schools encourage (or at least do not discourage) young boys to play with baby dolls for, after all, they *will* probably be fathers some day. The most talked about toys of Christmas '76 were the "anatomically correct" boy baby dolls.

It is particularly interesting that the justification for the baby boy doll's realistic anatomy is that it is little boys who have been confused by the lack of it through the years! Boys—and we were always lead to believe that it was little girls who played with dolls! Actually, little boys have always liked dolls, too, but no one wanted to admit it. It took two generations for two soft, cloth toys—Teddy and Andy— to pave the way for a whole new attitude towards dolls in our society.

There is another kind of doll becoming popular in America today—the artist's original doll. There seems to be some disagreement among the artists themselves about whether they are crafts, folk art, or fine art (I think all three), but they are coming into their own as an art form. These artists also are working on new definitions for the word "doll" which the dictionaries still call a "child's toy baby." While the doll artists are trying to decide what the difference between a doll and a figurine or statue is, it is appropriate to point out here that sculptors today are painting and putting real

6

clothes on their statues! Several large exhibitions recently in major cities in the U.S., by nationally-known sculptors and artists, have shown what many doll artists and collectors consider to be dolls.

Maybe some day doll-making will be considered the fine art in America that it has always been in Japan. We are at least moving in that direction.

The very idea of a doll that we mustn't touch, standing stiffly with its feet forever fastened to a base, has always left me cold. I consider them figurines, not really dolls! A doll need not be soft, although I prefer them that way, nor even flexible. I've loved many a stiff little doll whose legs were not even separated, but a doll, to me, should "stand on its own two feet." What I mean is that it should stand on its own merits because it can retain its character in any position or condition. If it must be frozen in one position in order to retain its character it is a statue.

My baby doll, for instance, feels like a baby, sits and lies down like a baby and even lets his legs fall in characteristic baby positions when you change his diaper and dress him. The way he *acts* is as much a part of the statement he makes as his looks.

A doll should be touched, held, squeezed, and enjoyed with as many of our senses as possible. Not only do we enjoy looking at him but we can find great enjoyment in touching him. With a littly baby powder in his diaper or a sachet in his stuffing, we can enjoy having him smell like a baby, and there are doll supply houses which sell "cry" or "talk" boxes to sew inside dolls to increase our enjoyment through the sense of hearing as well! A doll should not only be enjoyed through one's hands but cradled in one's arms or neck and rubbed against one's cheek and shoulder. The sense of touch *must* be explored to fully enjoy a doll.

If you have ever been to a doll show you must surely have been conscious of the strict rules against touching. There are ropes to keep people beyond arm's length and hostesses and guards everywhere to keep viewers back! Look but don't touch! How all of us yearn to reach out and feel the soft curls, run our fingers over a delicate face and explore the little hands and fingers! We know of course that all those hands could ruin the dolls; we understand *why* we can't touch but we can't help wanting desperately to do it anyway.

Only the very youngest of children "walk" a doll, talk to it, and actually role-play with it. Older children and adults "play" with a doll by holding it, hugging it, dressing and undressing it, arranging its hair, and mostly, when you come right down to it, just enjoying the way the doll *feels*.

If you observe in a store how people purchase a doll, you will be aware of the importance of the sense of touch in the selection. Dolls are usually displayed quite prominently for all to see but when a buyer, male or female, is making a decision, what do we hear? "Let me *see* that one," a customer will say, reaching out a hand. Mind you, the dolls can all be seen perfectly well. "Seeing," in this respect, means touching the hair, the face, lifting the skirts, and turning the doll around. "Let me *see* that one," means "I want to *touch* that one, to see how it feels, to enjoy it."

Some of the dolls you see photographed here have been held and hugged by my friends for three years! The two puppedoll babies and puppedoll child in Plate 5, and the babies in Plates 10, 11, and 12 have not only been held and hugged and played with but even slept with by my three-year-old grandniece and several young guests. My young friends are always allowed to enjoy these dolls during frequent visits to the Worrell house.

The rag doll, like the Teddy bear, is capable of inspiring genuine affection and loyalty from its owners. If dolls could feel—some believe they do—and tell of their feelings, they probably would choose the fate of being loved to pieces over that of spending a life attached to a base.

1. My American Children Series

"My American Children" series of cloth dolls includes four ages of children from an infant to a young girl. It all started three years ago when I went through our picture albums to study photographs of my children as babies for a baby doll I planned to design. My son, Sterling, was so pleased to discover me doing sketches from his baby pictures that he began calling the designs "Sterling dolls." My baby doll just naturally became Sterling and has remained so to all the family.

As I studied the way a child grows and his proportions change, I went through more albums until, in a few weeks, my "family" had evolved.

The baby Sterling in overalls in Plate 1 has my son's brown eyes and blonde hair. He also has his little left hand raised because Sterling is left-handed. Clare, the toddler, in Plate 2, was a chubby, dimpled cherub with platinum blonde hair. For several years as her hair turned chestnut brown, she had what she used to call striped hair because of its streaks. Beth, my only brunette baby of the four, has always worn her shining brown hair quite long while Anne's soft, blonde, natural curls have always attracted attention, even now as a college student. All three of the girls inherited their father's beautiful, long, dark eyelashes so the dolls, of course, have long eyelashes too.

Although not portraits, my children dolls do possess something of my own children's characters and general physical appearances. They are more impressions than portraits.

The portrait of my original American Children, Plate 9, shows "Lilibeth" the puppedoll child (left, rear). Although I also made an Elizabeth child doll, Plate 3, to my family the *real* Lilibeth will always be this one.

After I decided to write about my dolls, I made a new, fresh, clean Sterling baby to use instead of this well-worn one. He has been enjoyed by so many children and adults that his little hands are dirty! When I made the new one my children all looked at him and said, "That's not Sterling, *this* is Sterling," looking at my original baby. To them it would have been a deception to pass off the fresh, clean imposter for the real Sterling baby.

The bodies of the three younger children vary in length but not in width. The arms and legs, too, get longer as the children get older. With only small adjustments in length the clothing for the three can be interchanged. The girl doll, Anne, has more mature proportions and cannot share the clothes with the younger ones without more extensive adjustments. (Plate 10)

For several years a young child stays the same in measurements while all the time growing in height. I used to let out the hems of my daughters' skirts as they grew. I learned to take the sash and make a sewn-in belt in order to drop the waistline down. With three daughters to sew for I learned a lot about how children grow! I eventually began putting tucks in both bodice and skirt so all I had to do as they grew was take out a tuck and cover the evidence with braid or lace, if necessary.

Several years ago my dear friend, Betty Everett, had given me a large bound volume of *St. Nicholas Magazine* for children. In 1905 her parents had all the issues for the years 1903 and 1904 put into a thick leather and gold binding. I have used the volume for research many times and never cease to enjoy it and discover something new. One day while leafing through the brittle pages, I came upon the following poem of "The O'Callahan Picnic Gowns" which can illustrate for you, better than any anatomy lesson, how a child grows!

Top:

Plate 1. THE BABY DOLL. Sterling wears a cotton knit shirt and overalls, while Jenny wears an eyelet embroidery christening dress. Both have fur cloth hair and plain embroidered faces. Laurie, in a batiste dress and bonnet, has a contoured face and eyelashes. Her hair is made from a vinyl wig.

Bottom:

Plate 2. THE TODDLER DOLL. Clay wears short pants and sweater. Clare wears a party dress of batiste. Clay has fur cloth hair and a cloth built-up nose. Clare has human hair and "real" eyelashes.

9

Left, top:

Plate 3. THE CHILD DOLL. Elizabeth, with embroidery floss hair and "real" eyelashes, wears a modern cotton dress. Amy is dressed in a dainty Colonial dress and mob cap. Her hair is synthetic vinyl, her nose of built-up cloth.

Left, bottom:

Plate 4. THE GIRL DOLL. Anne, wears an old-fashioned dress with antique lace and buttons. Melissa wears a modern square-dance dress. Both dolls have "real" eyelashes. Anne has a cloth built-up nose, Melissa a felt contoured face.

Top:

Plate 5. THE PUPPEDOLLS. Puppedoll Child, Lilibeth, wears a gingham dress, pinafore, and sunbonnet. The Puppedoll Toddler, Happy, wears sleepers with matching blanket. Puppedoll Baby Estee's blanket and sacque have matching crochet edges as do those of Puppedoll Little Baby, Christopher. Both babies have hair of fur cloth; Lilibeth, of embroidery floss; and Happy, a hair wig.

Bottom:

Plate 6. THE TEDDY BEAR FAMILY. Pabear has a crochet cap and muffler and Mabear wears a dress and apron. Babear is dressed like his Pabear in cap and muffler. All have their fur clipped on their ears, noses, and paws.

Plate 7. THE FASHION DOLLS can be dressed in any period styles. Here a woman, Ruth, is dressed in an 1890s Gibson Girl skirt and blouse. The girl, Dorothy, and the child, Ann, are dressed in basic dresses. All three have embroidery floss hair.

Plate 8. THE OLD TIMEYS. Annie Mary is reminiscent of a kid-bodied papier-mâché doll and Lucy, of a wax doll. Viola with her straight body and painted hair suggests an old wooden doll.

Plate 9. MY AMERICAN CHILDREN are shown here as I originally created them to represent my own four children. Baby Sterling sits on the left while Toddler Clare stands beside him. In the rear is Lilibeth, the Child, left and Anne, the Girl, right.

Plate 10. The basic blank bodies of My American Children series show the dolls' body proportions. They are made of cotton/polyester broadcloth.

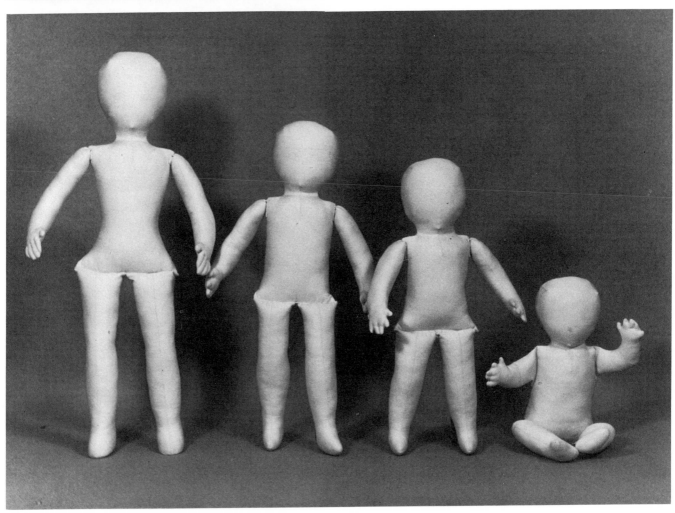

THE O'CALLAHAN PICNIC GOWNS.

By O'Ryan O'Bryan.

"Oh, Evelyn May,"
Said her mother, one day,
"Your gowns you are outgrowing quite;
So far as I see,
They 're as whole as can be,
And the colors are perfectly bright."

Now Evelyn May
Had her gowns made this way—
With four tucks running right round the waist.
The dresses were sweet
And exceedingly neat,
With colors in excellent taste.

Of pinks there were two,
And one red and one blue,
And a dainty white guimpe went with each;
But she 'd grown up so tall,
Not a belt of them all
To her slim little waist-line would reach.

"Please give them away,"
Said Evelyn May,
"And of Mrs. O'Callahan's four,
Surely one they will fit,
And I do hope that it
Will be dear little Bridget Lenore."

———

'T was the night before the picnic that the
gowns were sent away,
And the girls of the O'Callahans had had a
wretched day,
Weeping loud and weeping long,
And the burden of their song
Was that not a child among them had a dress
fit to display.

When the four had eaten supper and gone
sobbing up to bed,
And Mrs. Tim O'Callahan laid down her
weary head,
She was wakened from her nap
By a most tremendous rap
That, as Mrs. Tim declared, was "loud enough
to wake the dead."

At the package handed to her she was very
much amazed;
Then she lifted out the dresses, and her hands
to heaven she raised.
"Just look at that," she said;
"See the pinks, the blue, the red!
There is one for every child, may the saints
above be praised!"

When the gowns were out of pack
She was taken quite aback
That their lengths were all the same as they
lay upon the floor.
But she took the one of red;
"This I 'm very sure," she said,
"Will just suit my little Bridget, the O'Calla-
han No. 4."

Then her eye lit on a tuck.
"Now if I am not in luck!
I can lengthen out another just as quick as
quick can be."
So she added inches two
To the little gown of blue,
Laid it down beside the other for O'Callahan
No. 3.

Seeing that her hand was in it,
'T was the work of but a minute

To rip out as many tucks as she thought would
    make it do.
    Thus the pinkest of the pink
    Was let down in just a wink,
The four inches that were needed for O'Calla-
    han No. 2.

    The last one was so pretty
    It seemed a dreadful pity
That her daughter Mary Ann was to height in-
    clined to run;
    " But when all four tucks," said she,
    " Are let out, I 'm sure 't will be
A perfect fit for Mary Ann, O'Callahan No. 1."

On the morning of the picnic every child rose
    with the sun.
How they shrieked with joyous laughter when
    they saw what had been done !
    At the very stroke of eight
    They went sailing through the gate,
Little " Bridget L." O'Callahan and " 3 " and
    " 2 " and " 1,"
All ready for the picnic and quite eager for
    the fun.

BABY DOLL

The baby doll is about 15 inches tall and was inspired by my son, Sterling. He has curved legs and outstretched arms and is designed so that his hands will swing around to his face. His curved legs enable him to sit by himself. I often sew his two middle fingers down to the palm of his hand so that he points his index finger. Plates 2 and 19 of the little toddler boy show such a hand quite clearly.

Plates 15 through 18 show just a few of the many real-life positions my baby can take. He will provide endless hours of fun for anyone—especially someone with a sense of humor!

The darts at the wrists and elbows force the arms to curve in toward the doll. The ankle darts make the feet go up a bit in a natural position. The darts are for the front of the legs only. The doll is perfectly attractive without these darts so you can omit them on your first baby if you wish. In fact, if you are a beginning seamstress, I suggest that you do omit them on your first try or perhaps just try one dart in one arm. I made the discovery, when examining some of my antique dolls, that the fine quality ones often have arms and sometimes legs and even hands which are in different positions. When you do make one arm more curved than the other, you actually increase the number of positions your baby can take. I prefer to use the elbow darts in both arms with the wrist dart in only one. The wrist dart enables the baby to "suck his thumb" because it brings the hand in toward the face. (Plate 15) Topstitching at the shoulder line gives him flexibility. Two lines about one-quarter inch apart will enable his arms to swing freely and easily.

I have included patterns for a smaller eleven-and-a-half-inch doll that I call "Little Baby." It has patterns for a basic layette also. Young children particularly like this smaller baby. He is second from the right in Plate 14. In doll-playing if you use the child or girl dolls for "mother," he can be the "baby."

A still smaller doll, "Little Bitty Baby" is only seven-and-a-half inches tall. He can be the doll's doll, but I have observed that young children assume a baby is really much smaller than it is in proportion to adults so he, too, can be used for the doll's baby. He is on the far right in Plate 14.

Plate 14 shows a stair-stepped arrangement of five babies. The baby in the center is my basic fifteen-inch baby doll. On the left are two larger babies from the basic pattern enlarged on a graph. The largest baby on the left is twenty inches tall and large enough to wear newborn to three-month size real baby clothes. She has been used by local theater groups as a baby in stage productions. How much more convincing she is than those stiff plastic dolls I've seen in some stage plays! She has also been used in a local training class for parents-to-be because holding, dressing or diapering her is so close to the real thing.

Plate 11. Baby Stevie wears yellow cotton flannel sleepers. His hair is yellow fur cloth; his body is one-hundred-percent cotton. The sleepers are made in one-piece and button in the back.

To enlarge a pattern, draw your baby pattern on a graph with each square 1 inch in size. Draw, on a large piece of paper, a graph with squares 1¼ inches for the 1¼ size baby and 1⅛ inch squares for the 1⅛ size baby, second from the left.

The second baby from the left is about 17 inches tall. Normal babies range in height from 18 to 23 inches at birth. Since the dolls have a smaller head and feet than a real baby, this doll represents a new-born baby in scale.

The baby layette includes patterns for a dress, christening dress, sacque, overalls, bonnet, two pairs of shoes, shorts or panties, T-shirt, and sleepers. By combining these patterns and using patterns from the toddler and child sections, you can make many outfits. Just a little imagination and you can make a sunsuit, diaper suit, swim suit, apron, slip, snowsuit, bathrobe, rompers, underwear, nightgown, and several different dresses. You can make period styles, too, such as the little Colonial outfit shown with the Baby Doll pattern. I made a baby like this for a friend in 1976 and called her my Bicentennial Baby.

Basic dress skirt size for the baby is 8 by 40 inches.

16

Plate 12. Baby Shirley is felt and has a contoured face, eyelashes, and russet hair. She wears a slip made from the pinafore pattern.

Plate 13. Baby Alex models a blue sacque edged in white crochet, diaper, and high-topped shoes. He is made of brown felt with black fur cloth hair.

Plate 14. A stair-stepped arrangement of babies, from left to right, includes an enlarged 20-inch baby named Wendy, a 17-inch baby named Davy, 15-inch Baby Estee, 11½-inch Little Baby Christopher, and 7½-inch Little Bitty Baby Gilley.

The christening dress skirt should be 14 by 36 inches. I use either cotton flannel or bird's-eye diaper cloth for diapers, 8 by 9 inches in size. You can cut down real disposable diapers to fit. The socks are infant size baby socks, purchased at the five-and-ten-cent store. I cut and sew them straight across with the smallest size stitch just above the heel. (Plate 5)

The cotton flannel receiving blanket, 18 by 18 inches, is crocheted around the edge to match the sacque, also shown in Plate 5. Little Baby's blanket is 12 inches square while Little Bitty Baby's is 9 inches square. I always make the blanket match the sacque.

In Plate 11 baby Stevie models yellow cotton flannel sleepers. Shirley models a slip made with the pinafore pattern in Plate 12, while Alex, a brown-skinned felt baby in Plate 13, models a blue sacque with a white crocheted edge. His high-topped, white shoes are tied with blue ribbon ties.

Patterns for the Baby doll and clothes are on pages 24 through 39.

TODDLER DOLL

The toddler doll is 17 inches tall, with a torso body only slightly longer than that of the baby with chubby arms and straight legs. Her legs are straight because she can walk now. She really can walk if you hold her from the back with your fingers around her torso under her arms and rock her gently from side to side as you move her forward. Her legs will swing alternately, making her appear to walk.

As on the baby doll, the arm darts are optional. The Clare doll in Plates 2 and 9 does not have darts in either arm or hand. The little boy, Clay, in Plates 2 and 19 has darts at the wrists and elbows, making his arms curve inward. The girl toddler, Merrill, in Plate 20 has darts in her left arm only, making it curve in. All the arms curve forward because that's the way they are cut; the darts make them curve forward and inward at the same time giving them a more lifelike position. The darts are for the inside arm piece only.

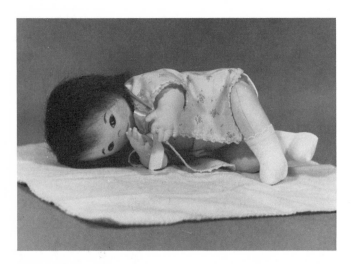

Plate 15. The Baby body is designed to take many lifelike positions. Here he (or she) lies on his side and sucks his thumb.

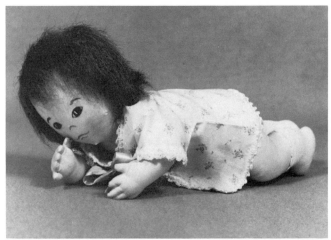

Plate 17. Baby lying on his tummy.

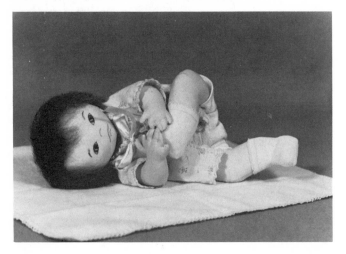

Plate 16. Baby playing with his foot.

Plate 18. Baby crawling.

Clothing for toddlers includes dresses, blazer or sweater, two pairs of shoes, coat, bonnet, and mittens. In combination with patterns for the baby and child you can add overalls, long trousers, panties, sunsuit, swimsuit, sunback dress or jumper, jacket, pinafore, slip, sleepers, snowsuit, nightgown, bathrobe, underwear, skirt and sweater, blouse or shirt and any number of period clothes.

Socks can be made from the tops of real baby socks while a sweater (Plate 2) can be made from a pair of adult-size knee socks. A stocking cap can be made from one adult-size sock.

Plate 19 shows toddler Clay in a blue Eaton suit. Merrill in Plate 20 models a deep pink coat and bonnet. Her mittens, missing from the photograph, are on a ribbon which goes through her sleeves in typical toddler fashion. She has a white fur muff, too! Barbara in Plate 21 models a red checked shirt with denim overalls. A puppedoll toddler, Happy, in Plate 5 models aqua cotton flannel pajamas and holds her blanket with its matching crocheted edge. With a brown or dark blue velvet collar and a belt in the back, the coat can become a boy's coat. A tiny wool check or tweed fabric is particularly fashionable. You can extend the front to make it double-breasted, too.

Patterns for the Toddler doll and clothes are on pages 40 through 47.

Plate 20. Toddler Merrill is felt and models a bright pink wool coat and bonnet. She has a hard face with a built-up nose and a hair wig on a wig cap.

Plate 19. Toddler Clay (also in Plate 2) wears a blue Eaton jacket with blue shorts. He has brown felt oxfords and real baby socks. Notice his hand with the pointing finger.

Plate 21. Toddler Barbara wears denim overalls and a red checked shirt. Her hair is a long, cream-colored fur cloth. She has a built-up nose and hard face.

CHILD DOLL

Elizabeth, the child doll, is about 18½ inches tall and represents the age when young children become so leggy. Her body and arms are slightly longer than those of a toddler, while her legs are longer by about one-quarter of the total length. The legs are one of the most attractive features of this basic doll.

As on the other dolls, the arm darts are optional. When used, they should be on the inside arm piece only. If you are a beginner, you might want to omit them. You can make this child "grow" a bit if you like by adding about an inch to the body and about an inch to the legs.

This doll is particularly well-suited for period clothes. With the patterns for the three children you can make her an Empire dress, a bustle dress and many more styles. With a variety of sleeves, bodices and necklines you can fashion her an outfit in just about any period you want. You can also make boy's clothes using the pants and blazer patterns. Kathy in Plate 22 models an old-fashioned, long-waisted dress of blue gingham, pantaloons, and sunbonnet. Shannon, a puppedoll child, in Plate 23, shows the long-waisted petticoat to go under the old-fashioned dresses.

Plate 22. The Child, Kathy, wears an old-fashioned blue checked dress with pantalets and sunbonnet. Her face is contoured; her hair is yellow embroidery floss.

Plate 23. The Child, Shannon, wears a long-waisted slip made from the long-waisted dress bodice pattern. Her hair is a long-pile fur cloth in a creamy platinum color.

Plate 24. The Child, Bryan, wears overalls and a long-sleeve cotton knit shirt. His hair is light brown fur cloth.

20

One of my favorite dolls, a boy named Bryan, models the overalls and long-sleeved knit T-shirt in Plate 24. In order to make them fit him, I lengthened the bib ½ inch and made the pants legs to fit. The T-shirt buttons at one shoulder. Plate 5 shows the puppedoll child, Lilibeth, in an old-fashioned gingham dress, batiste pinafore, lace-trimmed pantaloons, and sunbonnet.

Patterns for the Child doll and clothes are on pages 48 through 55.

GIRL DOLL

Anne, my eldest child, inspired this girl doll who is about 23 inches tall and has a more mature body than the three younger children. She can be dressed as a young girl, a teenager, and even as a woman, if you like. Her body has a more refined construction, having a separate piece to form the hips, rather than darts. Her feet have sewn in soles with several layers of cardboard inside to keep them firm on the sole.

The pattern shows her fingers closed and indicated by top-stitching, but I sometimes separate the index finger from the others.

It's interesting that the baby and toddler dolls have a way of looking very much "today"; it really takes some doing to make them look "period." The child and girl dolls are particularly well-suited to period looks although they can be very modern as well. This doll also is very easy to make into a portrait doll.

In Plates 4 and 9 my original Anne doll is made of a very pale pink percale to give her a fragile, old-fashioned look to go with the old-fashioned dress. Both the tulle lace and the crocheted buttons are antique. The modern Melissa in her red square dance dress in Plate 4 is made of peach-colored felt.

I had still another daughter, Raquel, who inspired the tawny-skinned favorite in Plate 25. She was a beautiful, foreign exchange student from Caracas, Venezuela who lived with us one summer. Raquel models a dress which is European in feeling, although not authentic, to illustrate how beautifully she adapts to any one of the many skin tones and nationalities which make up our world. I used a deep rosy-beige colored felt.

I had difficulty finding peach, pink, brown, and tan felt when I first started making dolls, but I eventually discovered that some fabric department managers will stock the skin colors for you if you point out to them that doll and puppet artists need them. One store near me ordered peach and beige at my suggestion and discovered that they sell these colors just as quickly as the bright colors! Remember that when you buy felt, it seems expensive at first but it is twice as wide as percale so you only need half as much. It comes out about the same cost per doll and you don't have to worry about cutting on the straight grain or bias.

Patterns for the Girl doll and clothes are on pages 56 through 64.

Plate 25. A Girl doll named Raquel wears a pink dress with a green felt over-bodice to give it a European folk look. Her skin is dark beige felt to illustrate that beautiful dolls can be made to represent any nationality or race.

2. Constructing the Dolls

THE PATTERN

When tracing your pattern, draw it as it appears on the page, *carefully drawing the center fold line.* If your paper is transparent, just flip it over and trace again on the other half, completing the pattern. If your paper is opaque, fold carefully on the fold line, pin or tape it in place to prevent the paper from slipping, and cut to complete the pattern.

The larger patterns such as the dolls' bodies and the pinafore had to be extended across two pages. Wherever this is done it is clearly noted on the pattern, ("join this edge to pattern on following page to complete") and on the following page ("join to pattern on pre- ceeding page"). So many readers have stated that they prefer half a pattern and even "broken" patterns to re- duced patterns. You have to trace them anyway, so it's no trouble to fold or flip the paper and you get a more accurate pattern besides. In my own private informal poll among quilters, craftsmen, and doll artists I dis- covered that they are impatient people who value every precious moment of their creative time. Everyone I polled expressed a dislike for reduced patterns which have to be mathematically enlarged before the reader can get down to work.

One of the most frequently expressed comments I hear as I meet readers around the country is, "I just love your book because I can use the patterns without having to read it!" This is often followed by a blush or a stammer as the person begins to explain that it was intended as a compliment. Well, I've always accepted it as a genuine compliment because I feel that pattern designs, like dolls, must stand on their own merits! You see, I'm a wife, mother of four, writer and artist, and I know the value of my creative time. I, also, hate spending precious time searching through a text for information to explain a vaguely labelled pattern.

I always make two leg and two arm patterns so that I can pin them on a double cloth and cut them in sets. *It is important, when making your pattern, that you label it properly and note the number of pieces you will need of each.*

Cut an extra doll's hand pattern from heavy paper or cardboard—just the hand and a bit of the arm—*eliminat- ing the seam allowances.* The only way to achieve beautiful doll hands is by drawing them onto the cloth and then sewing directly on the finger outlines or seam lines with a very small stitch.

CUTTING

Lay your patterns out and pin them in numerous places to prevent slipping. The more you pin, the more accurate your cutting can be. Some quilt and doll-makers I know use large corsage pins for this.

Marking your pieces as you cut is extremely important so that when you sit down to your sewing machine and begin to sew you won't have to go back to the cutting table to find out where the darts and top- stitching go or how the pieces fit together. I prefer to use a pink colored pencil for this because it doesn't show through the pink cloth at the seams like a regular lead pencil does. If you use a lead pencil, mark carefully but *lightly.* (If, when you stuff your doll, you discover that your pencil marks show on the fingers, you can clean it off with a bit of cotton or a cotton-tipped stick and a little soap and water.) Do not use crayons or felt- tip pens. The pink colored pencil can be used on dark- skinned dolls as well as the fair-skinned ones while the lead pencil can't.

You will need to trace your doll's face on *the opposite side of the front piece* from the other marks. This can be done with a regular pencil also, but here again, a pink pencil works beautifully. (This same pink pencil will be used later for the doll's cheeks.)

One of the most important marks you will use is the dot at the center top of the head: you start matching your pattern pieces from that point and go down each side when pinning and sewing together.

It is not necessary to mark all the clip marks on your cloth. They are on the pattern only to remind you where it is essential to clip. An experienced seam- stress already knows when and where to clip but the reader who has not made many cloth dolls before might appreciate being reminded where clips are needed.

SEWING

Sew all darts as marked. If you want the nice curve of the arm that the wrist dart will achieve, then baste your front and back pieces together before sewing. When basting, pinning, or sewing, *start at the dot at the center top of the head* and go down each side.

On all the Baby Dolls and "Babear" you secure your center dot by pinning, but start sewing at the head darts instead, and then go down the sides. The curved-leg babies are stuffed from the top of the head; the other dolls from the hips. Little Baby and Babear and Little Bitty Baby have the legs, body, and arms all in one piece. This does not include the smallest bear, Bitty Bear, who has sew-on arms and legs.

The Hands. When sewing around the fingers, adjust your machine to the smallest size stitch and sew directly on your pencil outline of the fingers. When you come down in between the separated fingers, *turn and go two stitches across* before turning and sewing up the side of the next finger. This is most important as you will see when clipping and turning later.

The Hips. The dart at the hipline can be just folded or pinned in place as you sew, making a tuck instead of a dart. Its purpose, of course, is to give the doll some fullness at the hips, both for looks and for sitting.

The Legs. The Baby Doll is sewn across the hips and crotch, completely closed across the bottom. This is because the angle of the legs is so important on this particular doll.

The doll's legs should be turned under and whip-stitched to the hips after stuffing. They work best when you hold the legs toward the front and sew from the back side.

The Arms. The Babies' arms are a part of the doll and are therefore sewn when the body is sewn. They are top-stitched later at the shoulders. The other dolls have separate arms with tabs for attaching them. This tab is sewn and turned so there are no raw edges. (The arm is stuffed from the back seam). Hold the arm in an up-raised position *with the tab going down.* Sew the tab by hand to the shoulder and down the side of the body. Sew securely at the top and then all the way around the tab. When this is neatly done, the arms have the look of a jointed doll and can be placed into many natural positions.

This method of attaching the arms enables your doll to wear sleeveless or bare-topped clothes, which is rare for cloth dolls.

Clipping. In sewing anything, clipping is an important part of the art. In dolls, it is *absolutely essential* to their beauty and accuracy. Clipping should be done after sewing. The clip marks on the patterns are just a reminder to you of where the clips are needed. They need not be marked on your cloth.

If you sew two stitches across at the base of the separated fingers the clipping will be successful. Accurate marking, sewing, and clipping will give your doll beautiful hands. In fact, the hands can't even be turned right-side-out without being clipped.

A clip in the chin dart is another absolute must! The chin simply won't work unless the dart is clipped at least once at its widest point. Smaller clips above and below that one will allow the chin and neck to curve properly when turned and stuffed.

STUFFING

I always start stuffing the dolls with the slowest part first, the fingers. I have used cotton batting and kapok but they will bunch and are bad for those of us with allergies. A one-hundred-percent polyester fiber trademarked "Poly-fill" is preferred by most doll makers I know. It retains its spring even when packed tightly. Dolls can be stuffed with old nylon stockings cut into small pieces, making a machine-washable doll! You will need to wrap the tiniest bit of stuffing around a small dowel stick or cotton tip stick and push it firmly into each finger. Pack them tightly, then the hands and then the arms, using larger amounts on a larger dowel as you go.

On the Baby-Doll body stop packing the arms at least a half-inch from the shoulders and pin a safety pin at the shoulder line indicated on the pattern. Pack the body firmly and stitch across the line where the pin was. This will give the arms room to come forward or move up or down.

I always do the finger top-stitching by hand as well as the shoulder and hip stitching on Little Baby, Little Bitty Baby, and Babear. My friend, Esther, who made the blank bodies in Plate 10 does all her top-stitching by machine. I use a single thread in a tiny back-stitch for the fingers and a small running stitch for the shoulders and hips.

Even though a cloth doll is beautifully designed in form, when making one, even from the most exquisite pattern, a certain amount of sculpturing should be done by hand.

Stuffing the doll very firmly is the first step in filling out the form properly. But, cloth has a great deal of flexibility and elasticity, especially on the bias. Three people can make the same doll from the same pattern and make each appear quite different. The firmer the doll is filled, the better and easier it is to sculpture.

Sometimes, after stuffing the doll, it may be quite lopsided because of the way the cloth has stretched. After stuffing, you can squeeze the arms and curve or straighten them so they don't wrinkle, curve the fingers and squeeze the hands to flatten them. The legs should be pressed from the sides at the knees and ankles, to enhance the shape, and the body smoothed and pressed so that it is perfectly formed and symmetrical. The head can be pressed with all your fingers from the back while you hold your thumbs at the temples, making the face round out nicely. I always do this after embroidering the face and adding the wig.

More detailed sculpturing can be done on the fingers with a large needle, rearranging the stuffing inside. The needle can be used to enhance the face as described in the next chapter.

BABY DOLL

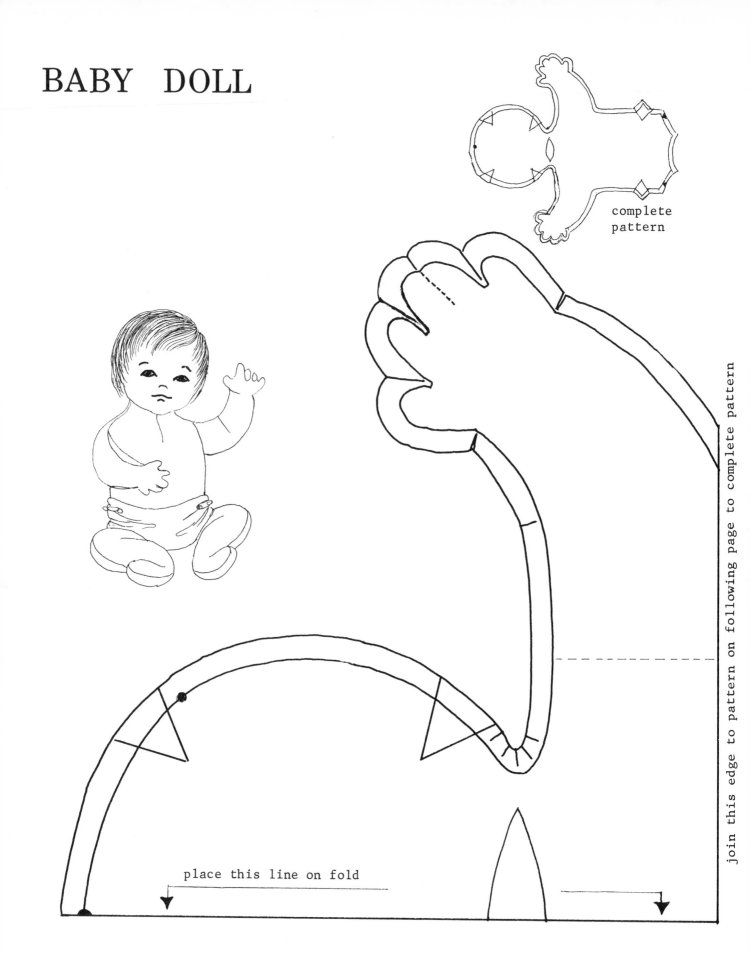

complete pattern

place this line on fold

join this edge to pattern on following page to complete pattern

24

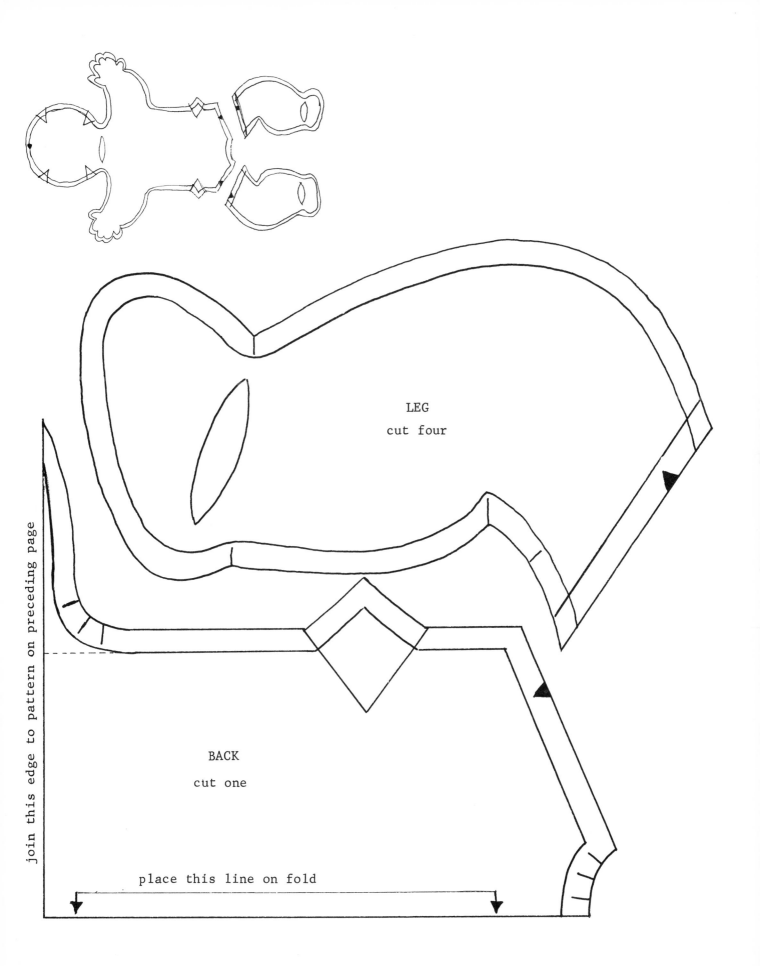

LEG

cut four

BACK

cut one

join this edge to pattern on preceding page

place this line on fold

BABY DOLL

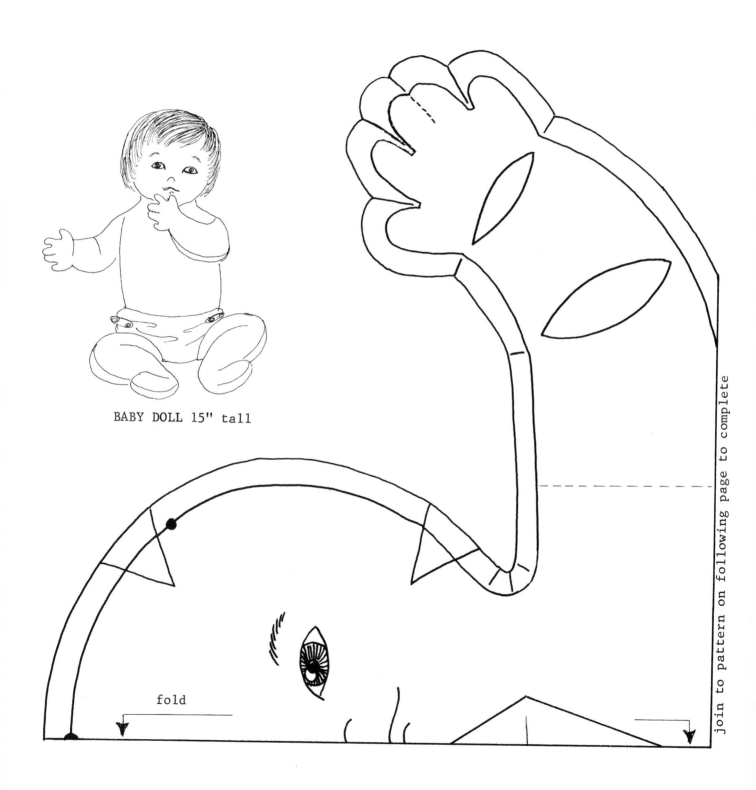

BABY DOLL 15" tall

fold

join to pattern on following page to complete

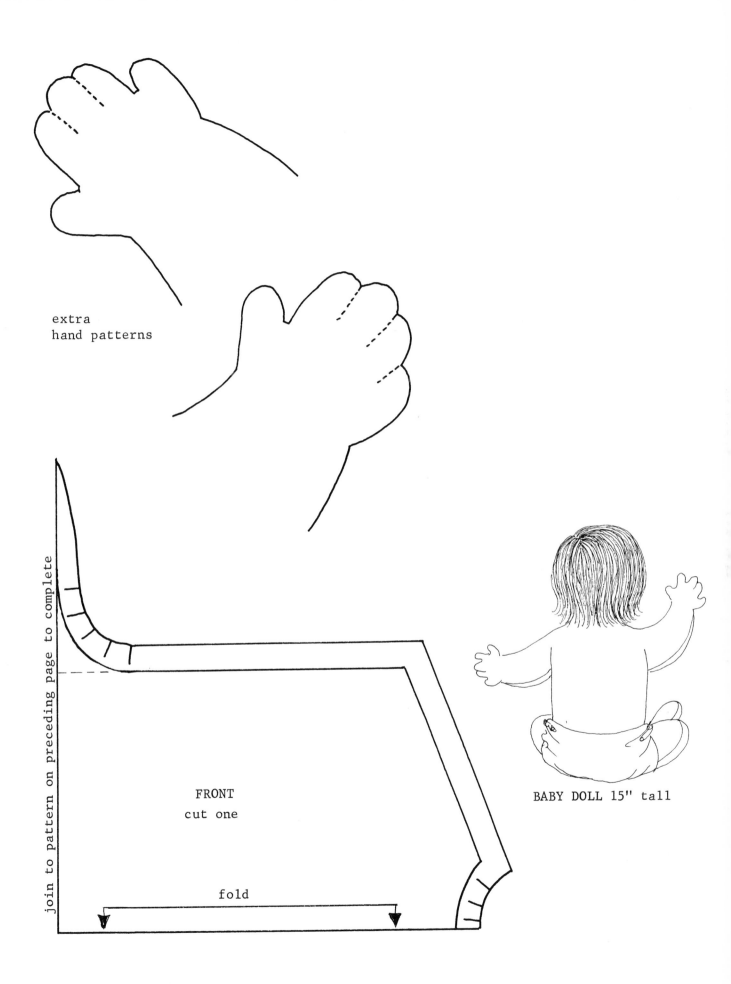

extra
hand patterns

join to pattern on preceding page to complete

FRONT
cut one

fold

BABY DOLL 15" tall

27

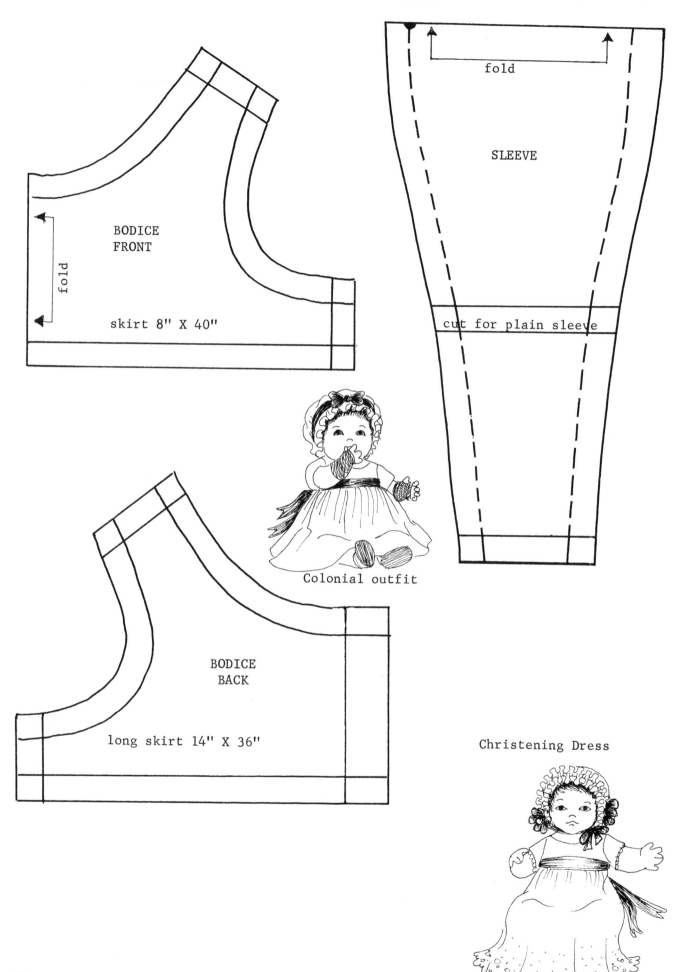

BODICE
FRONT

fold

skirt 8" X 40"

SLEEVE

fold

cut for plain sleeve

Colonial outfit

BODICE
BACK

long skirt 14" X 36"

Christening Dress

28

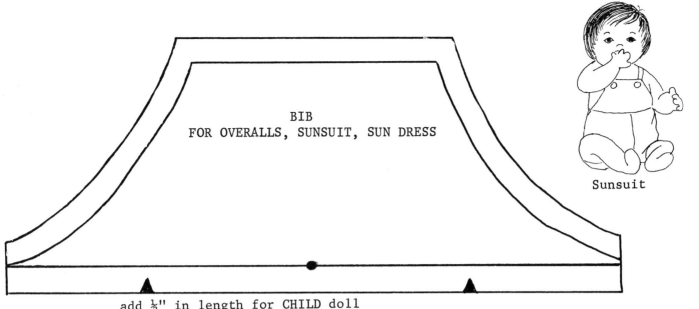

BIB
FOR OVERALLS, SUNSUIT, SUN DRESS

Sunsuit

add ½" in length for CHILD doll

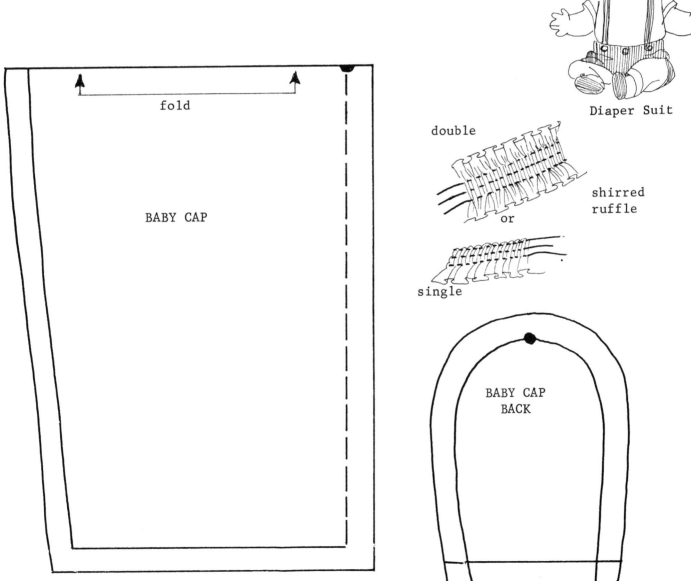

fold

BABY CAP

Diaper Suit

double

shirred
ruffle

or

single

BABY CAP
BACK

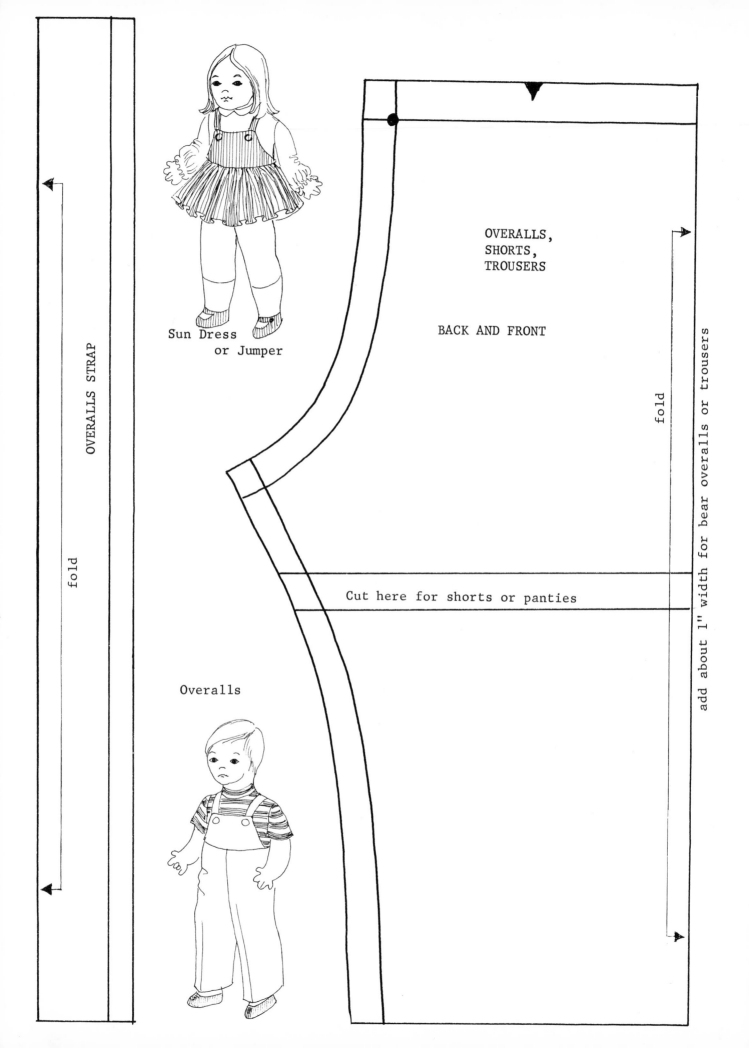

OVERALLS STRAP

fold

Sun Dress
or Jumper

Overalls

OVERALLS,
SHORTS,
TROUSERS

BACK AND FRONT

fold

Cut here for shorts or panties

add about 1" width for bear overalls or trousers

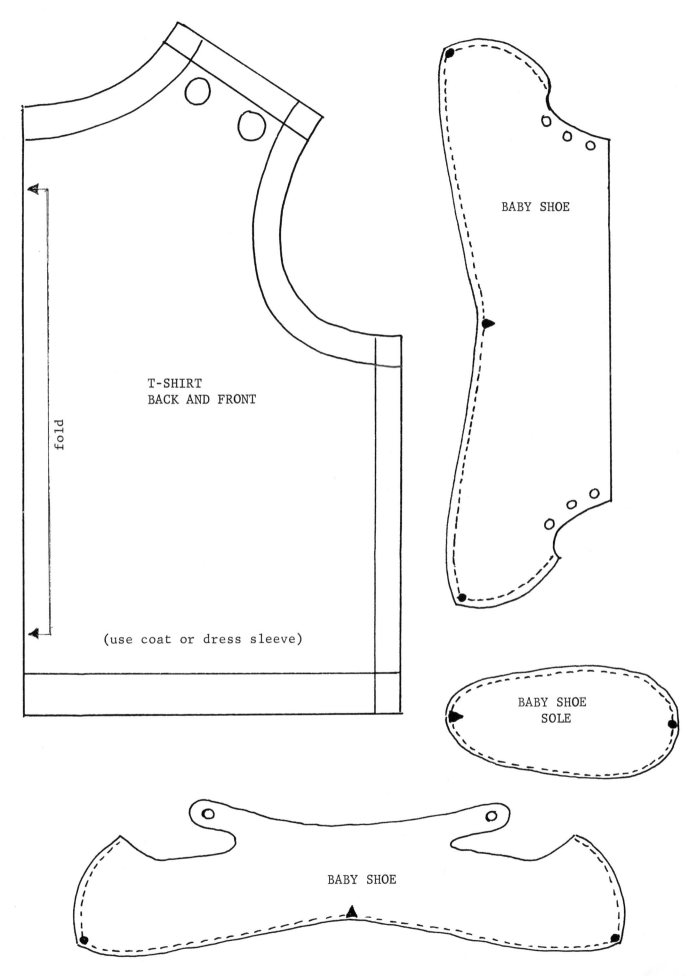

T-SHIRT
BACK AND FRONT

fold

(use coat or dress sleeve)

BABY SHOE

BABY SHOE
SOLE

BABY SHOE

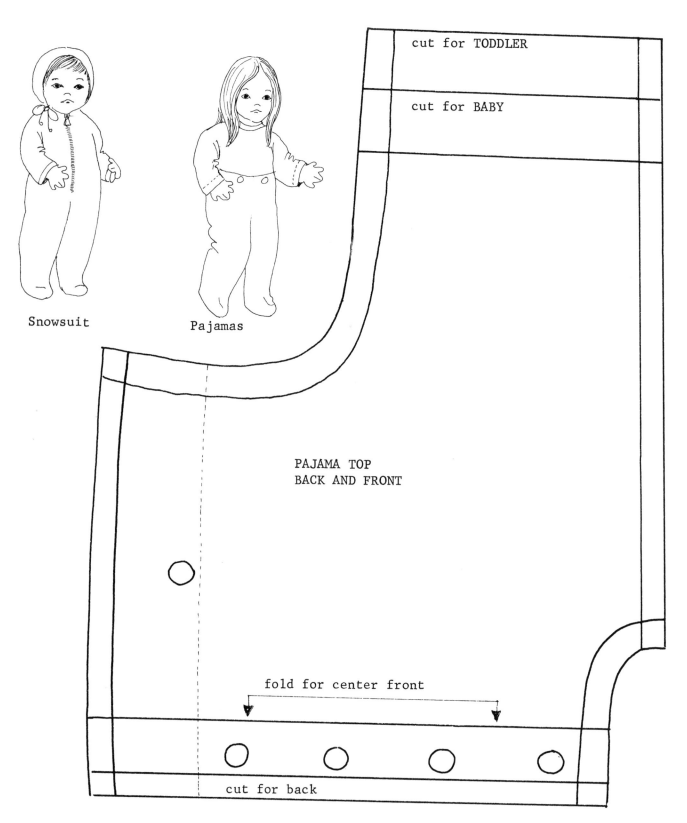

cut for TODDLER

cut for BABY

PAJAMA TOP
BACK AND FRONT

Snowsuit

Pajamas

fold for center front

cut for back

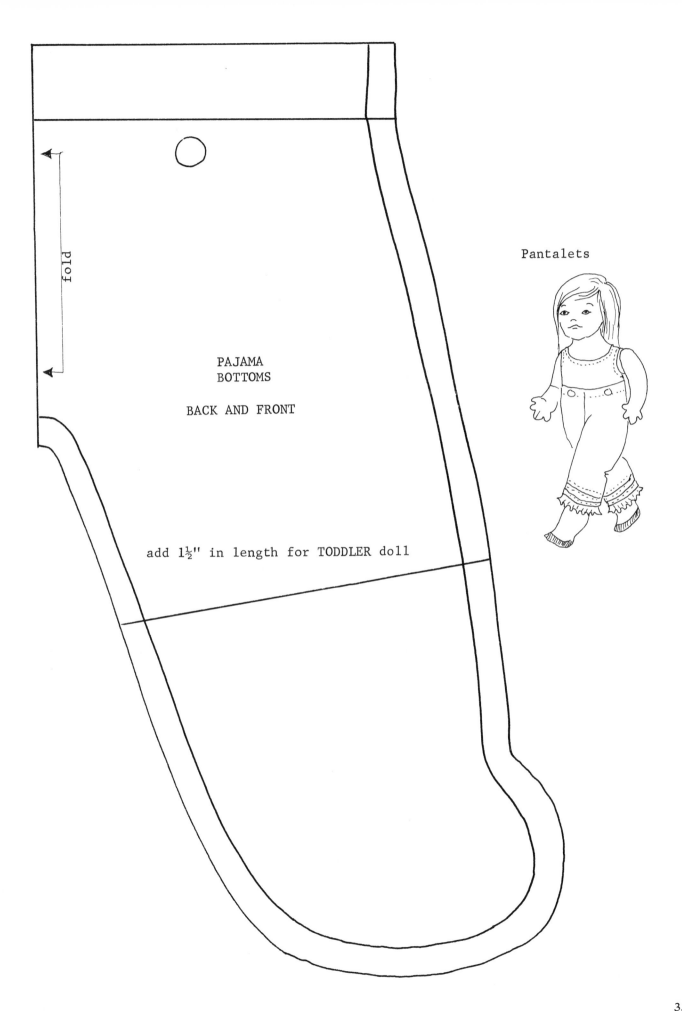

fold

PAJAMA
BOTTOMS

BACK AND FRONT

add 1½" in length for TODDLER doll

Pantalets

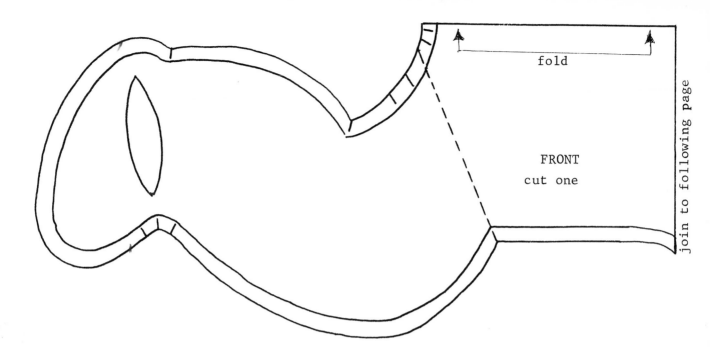

join to following page

fold

FRONT
cut one

LITTLE BABY

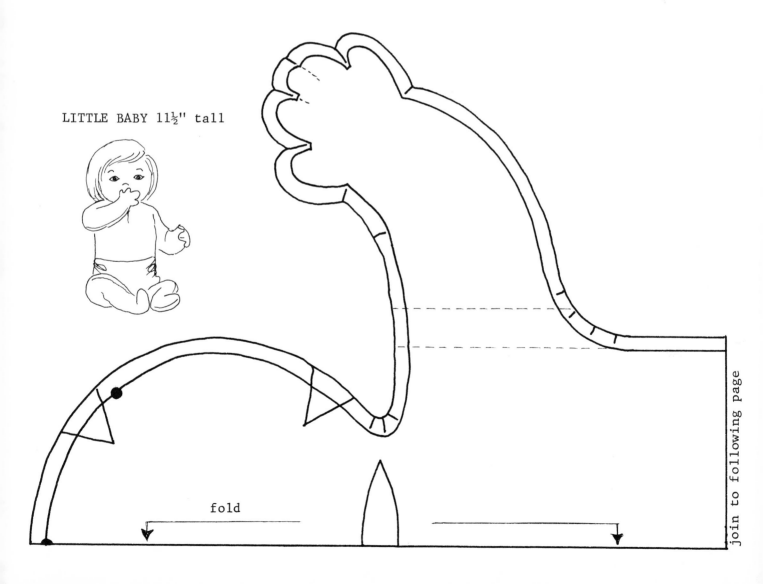

LITTLE BABY 11½" tall

join to following page

fold

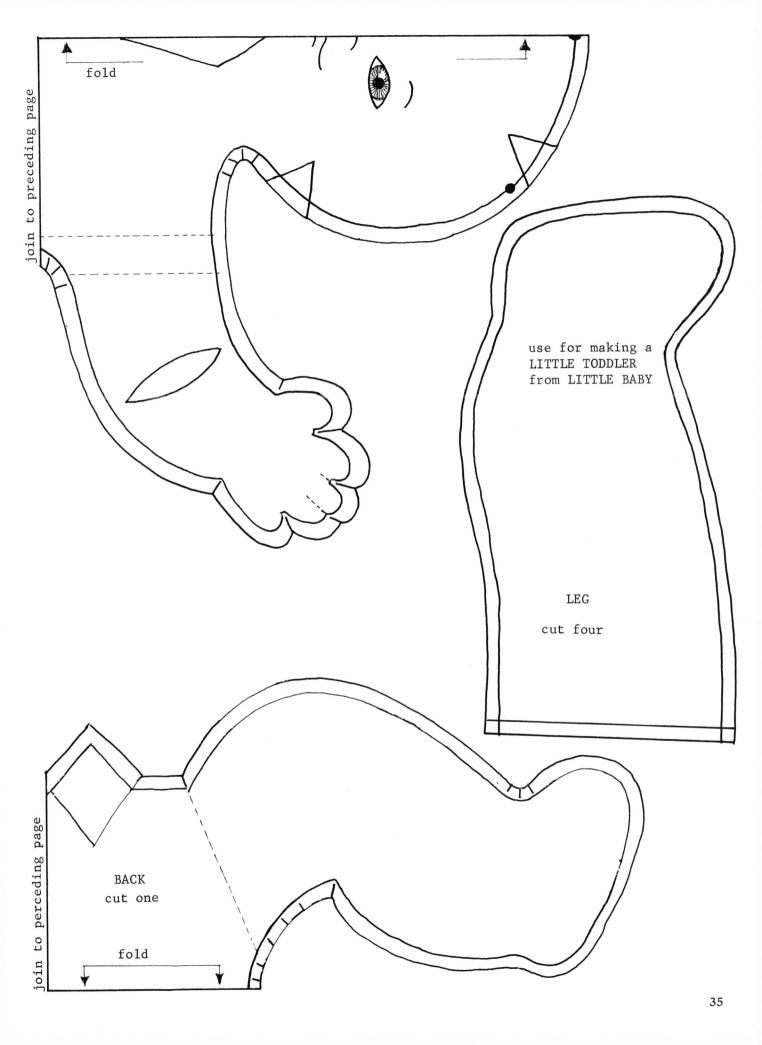

fold

use for making a
LITTLE TODDLER
from LITTLE BABY

LEG

cut four

BACK
cut one

fold

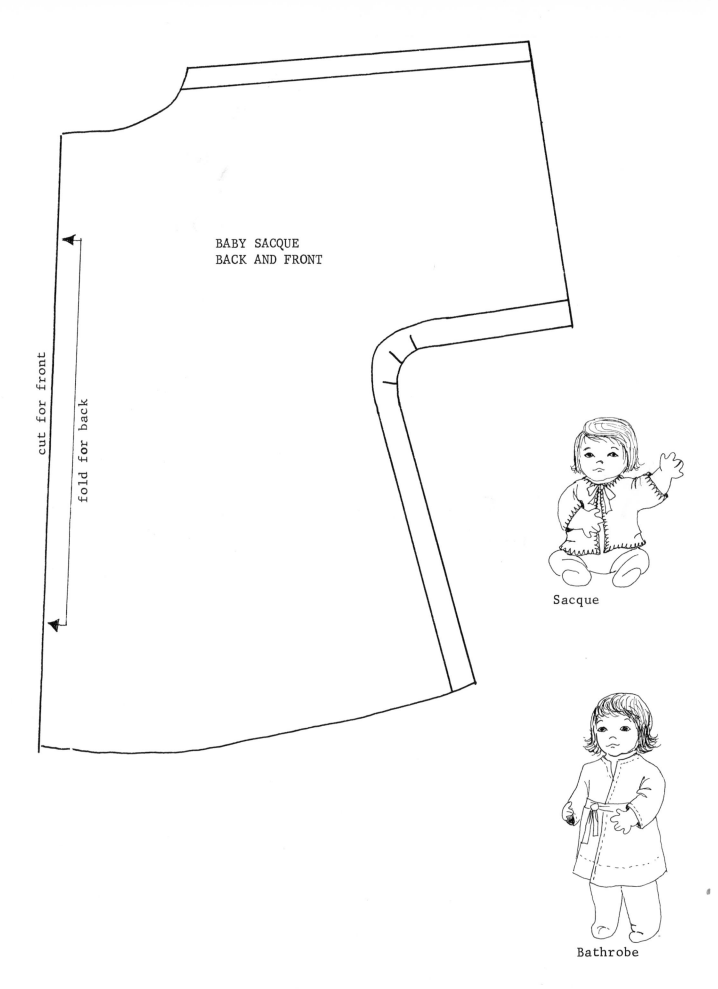

BABY SACQUE
BACK AND FRONT

cut for front

fold for back

Sacque

Bathrobe

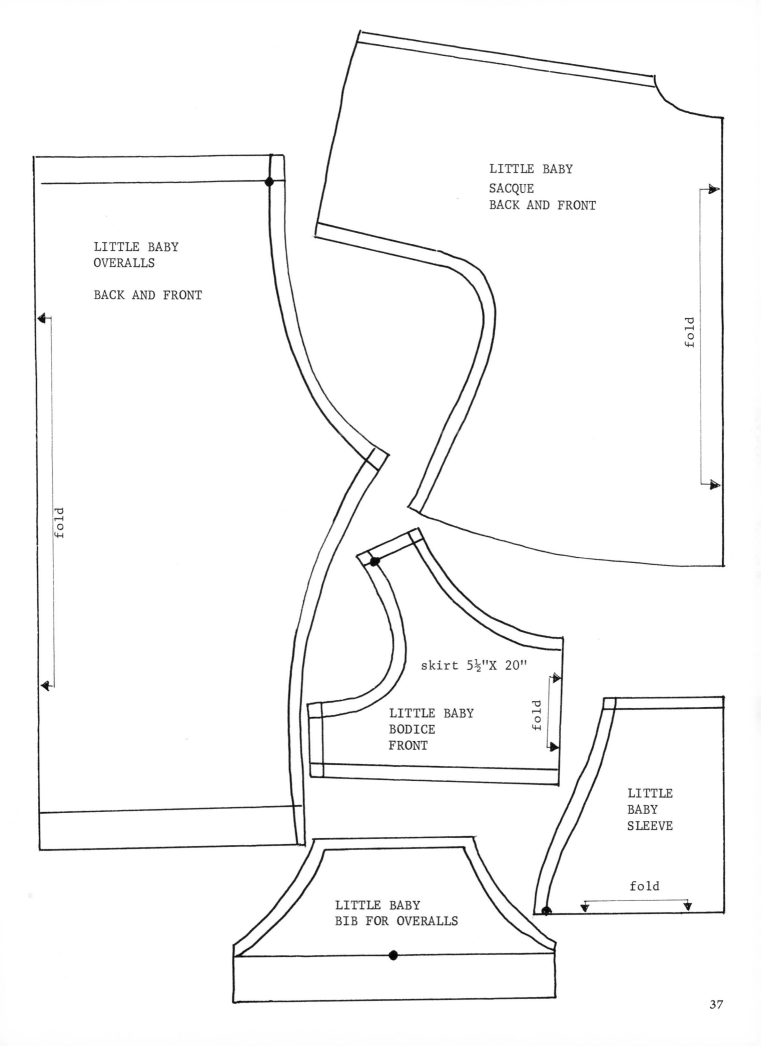

LITTLE BABY
SACQUE
BACK AND FRONT

fold

LITTLE BABY
OVERALLS

BACK AND FRONT

fold

skirt 5½"X 20"

fold

LITTLE BABY
BODICE
FRONT

LITTLE
BABY
SLEEVE

fold

LITTLE BABY
BIB FOR OVERALLS

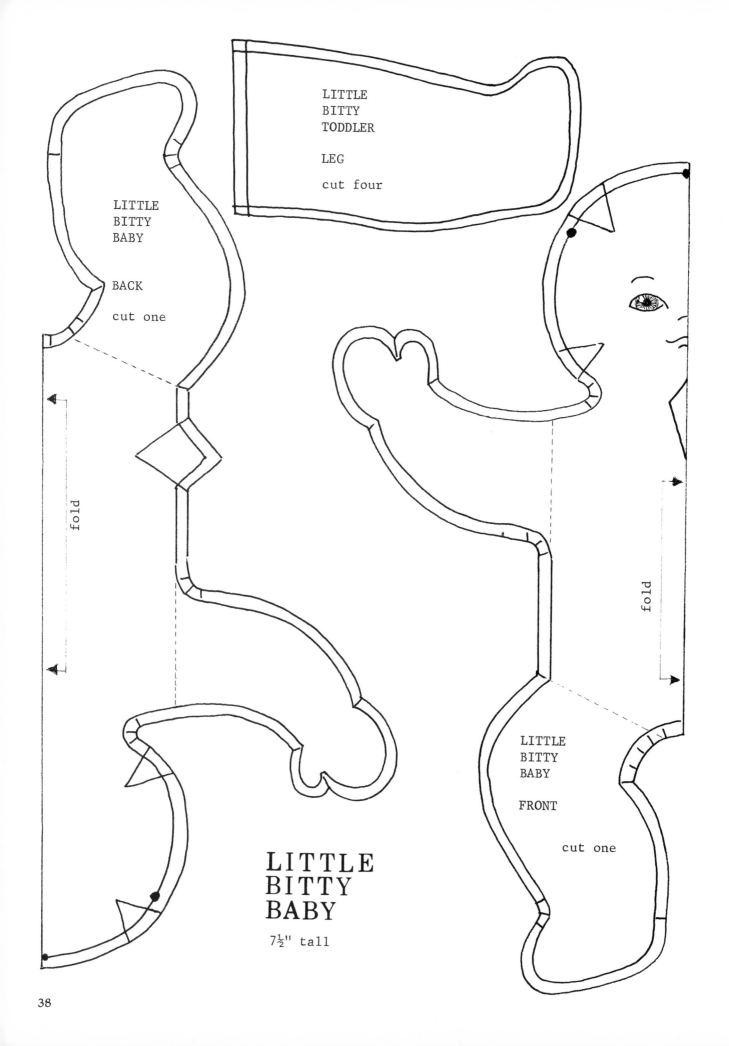

LITTLE
BITTY
TODDLER

LEG

cut four

LITTLE
BITTY
BABY

BACK

cut one

fold

LITTLE
BITTY
BABY

FRONT

cut one

fold

LITTLE
BITTY
BABY

7½" tall

38

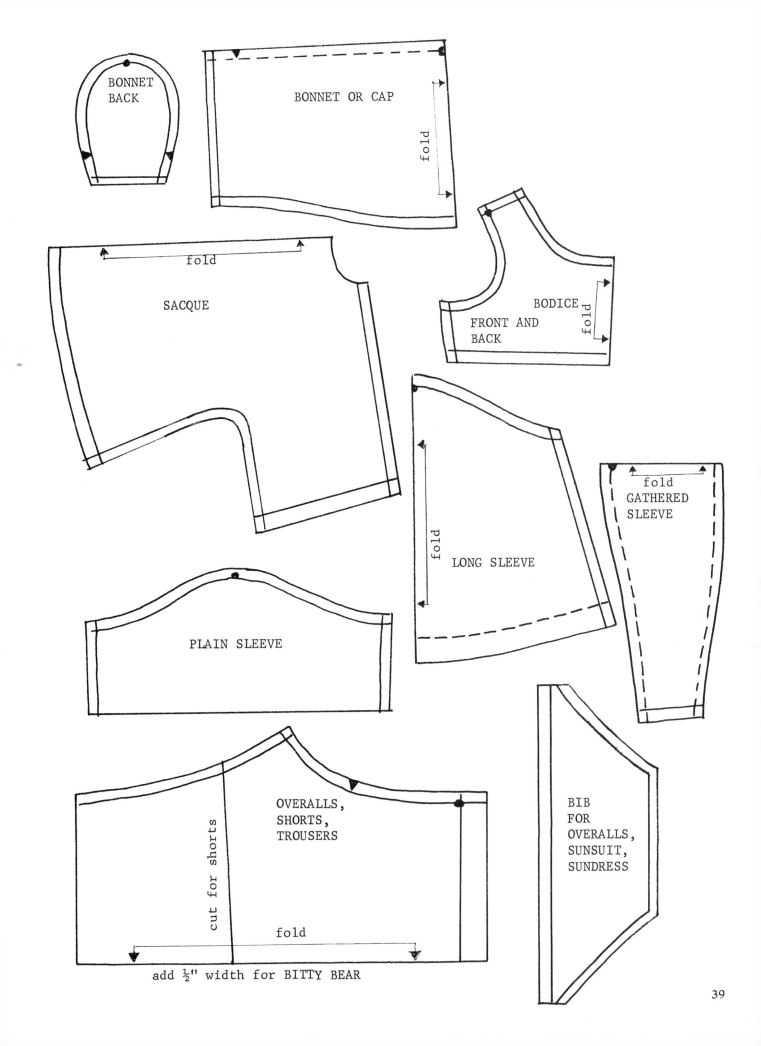

BONNET
BACK

BONNET OR CAP

fold

SACQUE

fold

BODICE
FRONT AND
BACK

fold

LONG SLEEVE

fold

GATHERED
SLEEVE

fold

PLAIN SLEEVE

OVERALLS,
SHORTS,
TROUSERS

cut for shorts

fold

add ½" width for BITTY BEAR

BIB
FOR
OVERALLS,
SUNSUIT,
SUNDRESS

39

TODDLER DOLL

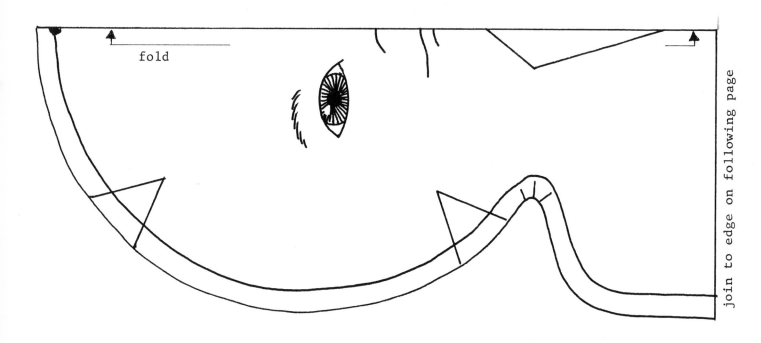

fold

join to edge on following page

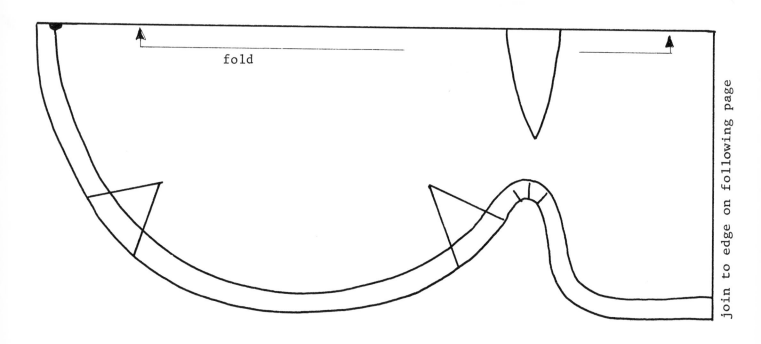

fold

join to edge on following page

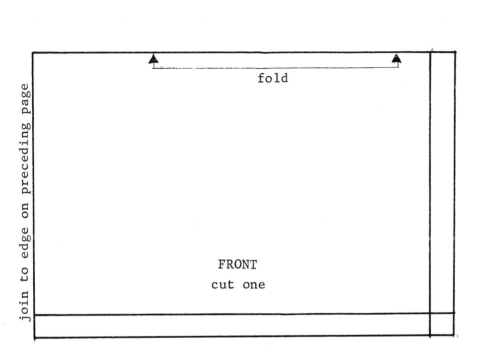

fold

join to edge on preceding page

FRONT
cut one

TODDLER DOLL 17" tall

fold

join to edge on preceding page

BACK
cut one

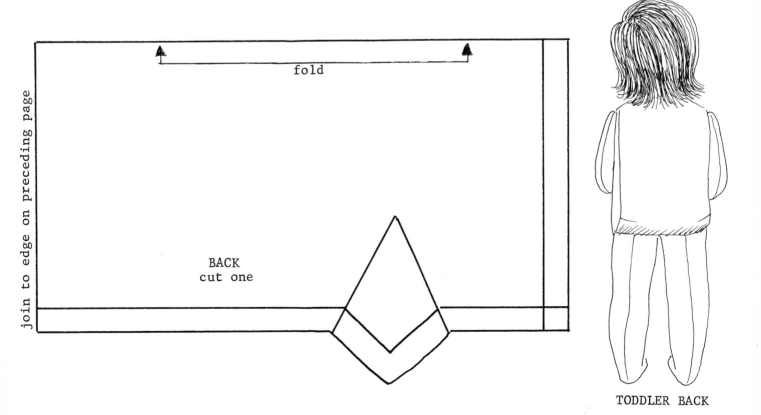

TODDLER BACK

TODDLER DOLL

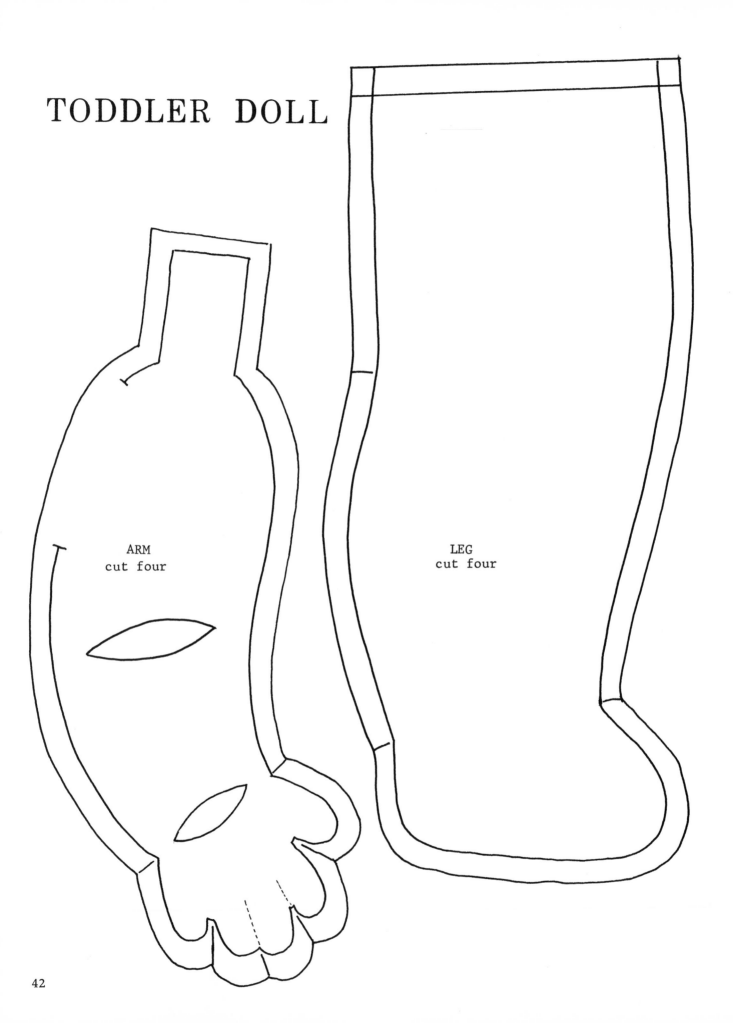

ARM
cut four

LEG
cut four

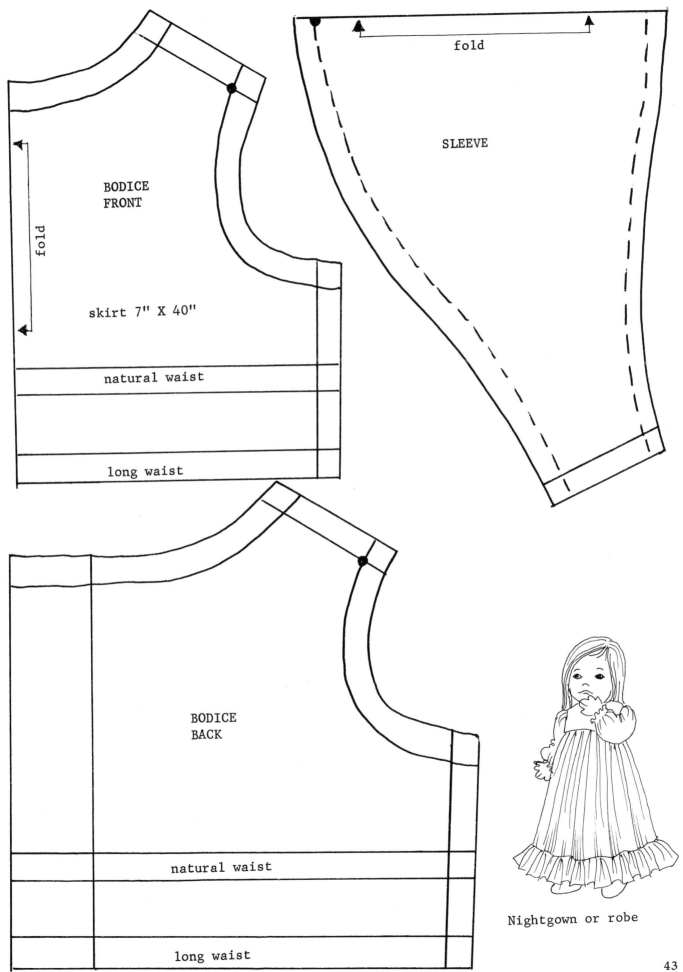

BODICE
FRONT

fold

skirt 7" X 40"

natural waist

long waist

SLEEVE

fold

BODICE
BACK

natural waist

long waist

Nightgown or robe

43

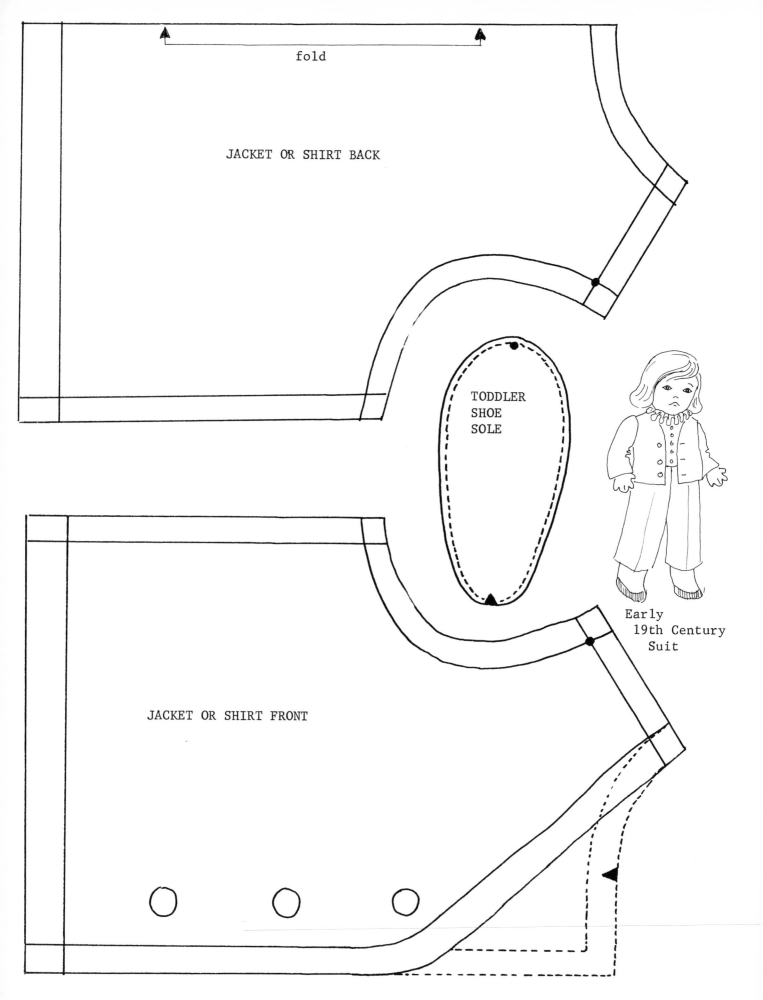

fold

JACKET OR SHIRT BACK

TODDLER
SHOE
SOLE

JACKET OR SHIRT FRONT

Early
19th Century
Suit

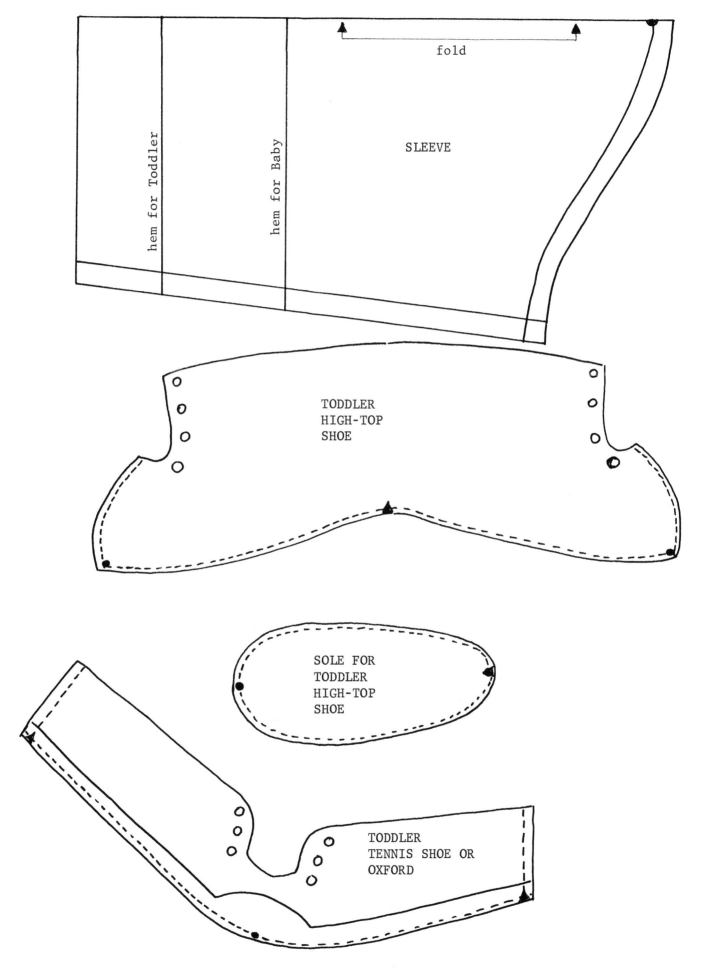

fold

hem for Toddler

hem for Baby

SLEEVE

TODDLER
HIGH-TOP
SHOE

SOLE FOR
TODDLER
HIGH-TOP
SHOE

TODDLER
TENNIS SHOE OR
OXFORD

45

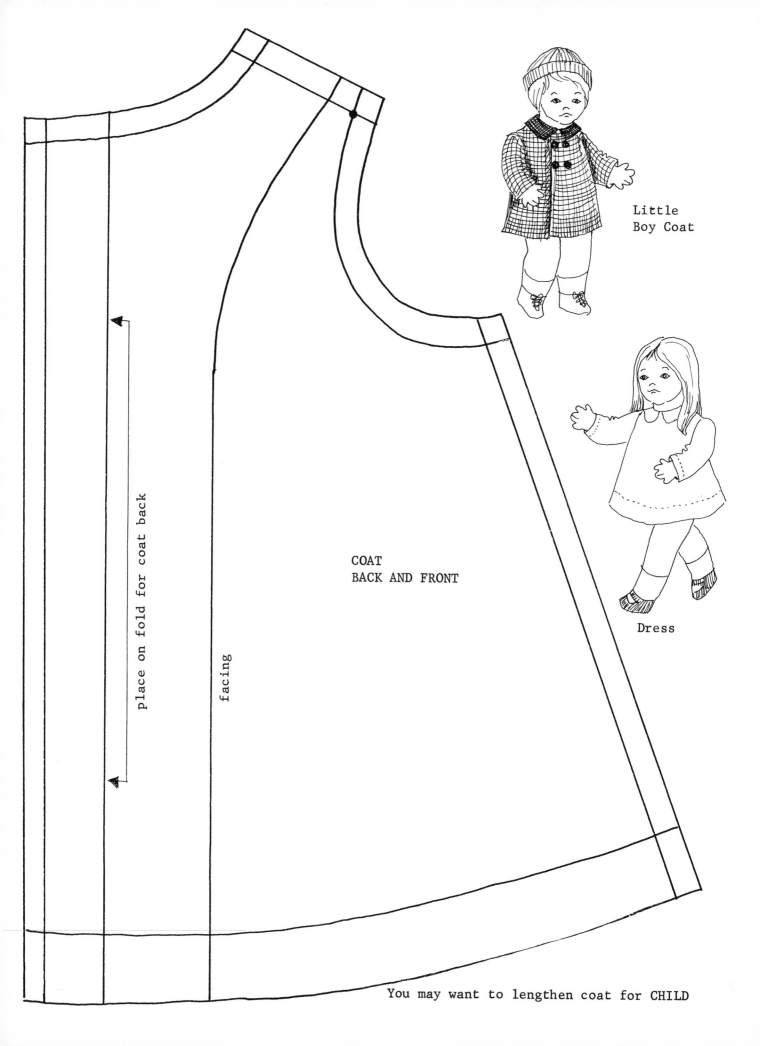

place on fold for coat back

facing

COAT
BACK AND FRONT

Little
Boy Coat

Dress

You may want to lengthen coat for CHILD

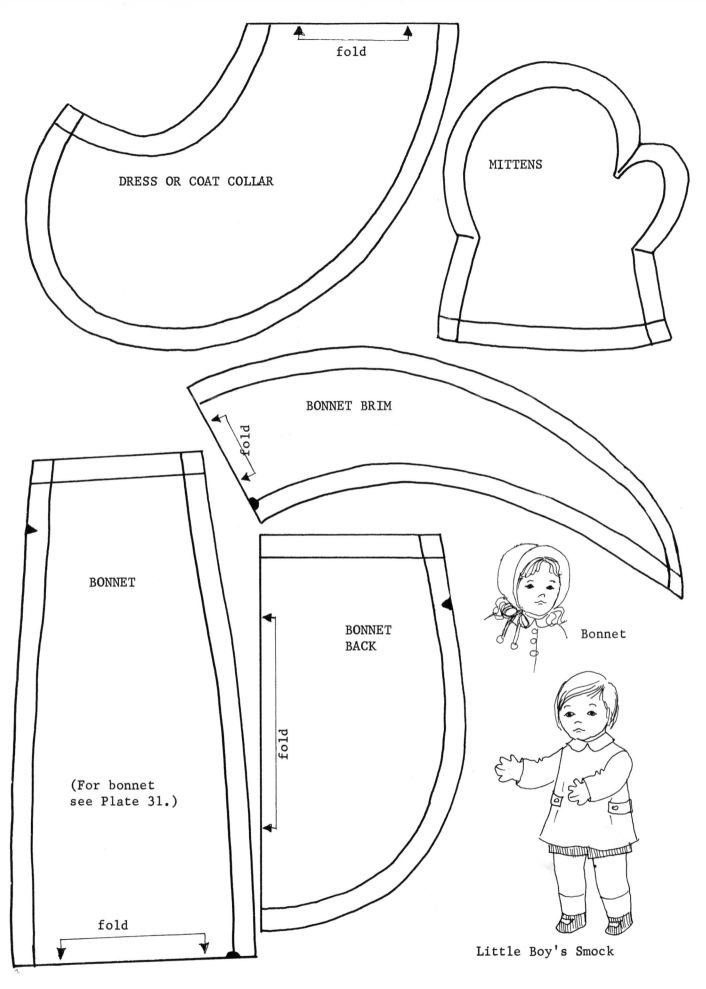

DRESS OR COAT COLLAR

fold

MITTENS

BONNET BRIM

fold

BONNET

(For bonnet
see Plate 31.)

fold

BONNET
BACK

fold

Bonnet

Little Boy's Smock

CHILD DOLL

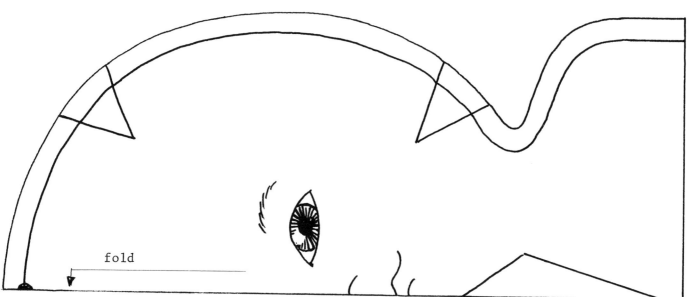

join to pattern on following page

fold

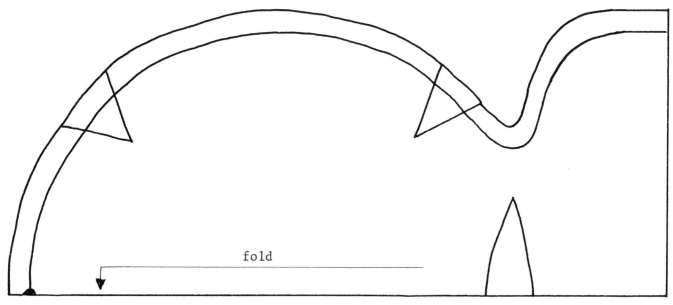

join to pattern on following page

fold

48

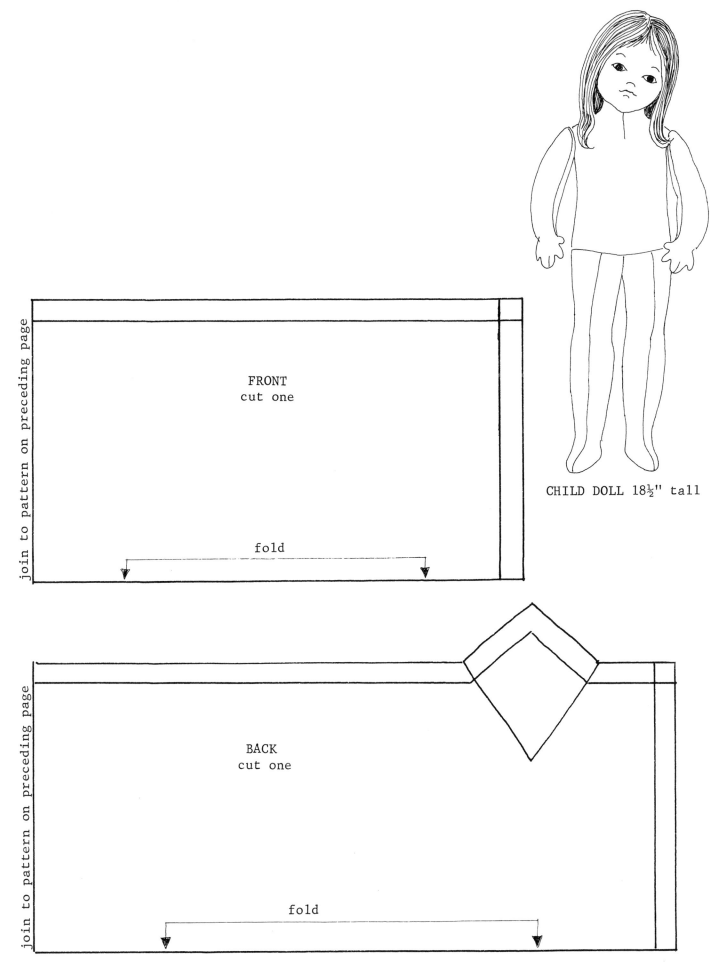

FRONT
cut one

fold

CHILD DOLL 18½" tall

BACK
cut one

fold

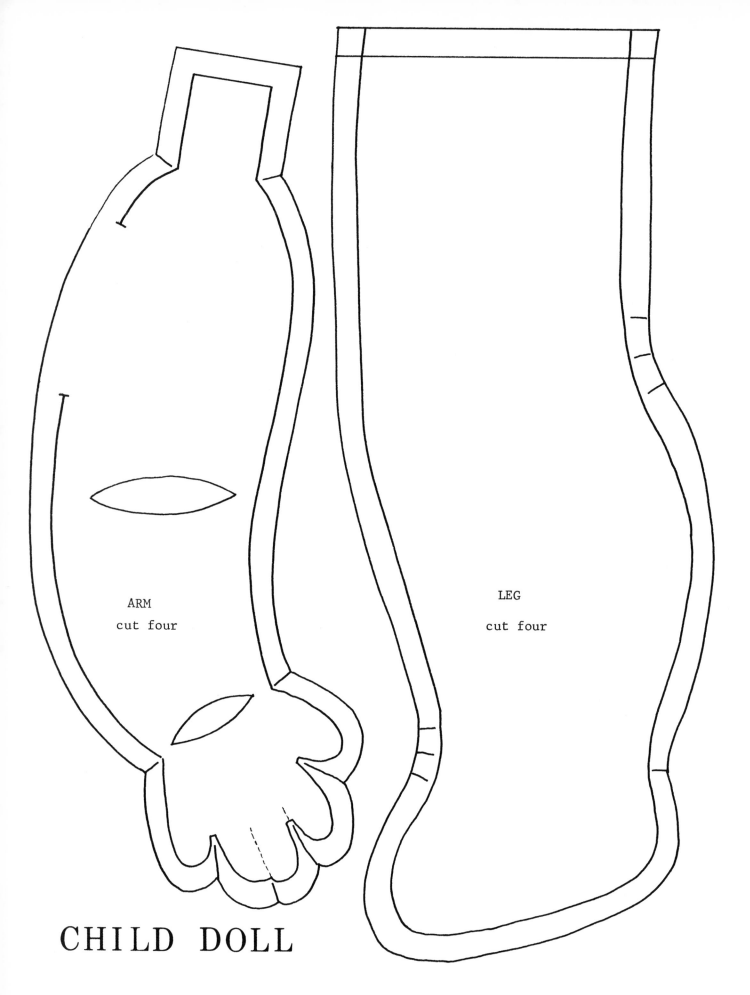

ARM
cut four

LEG
cut four

CHILD DOLL

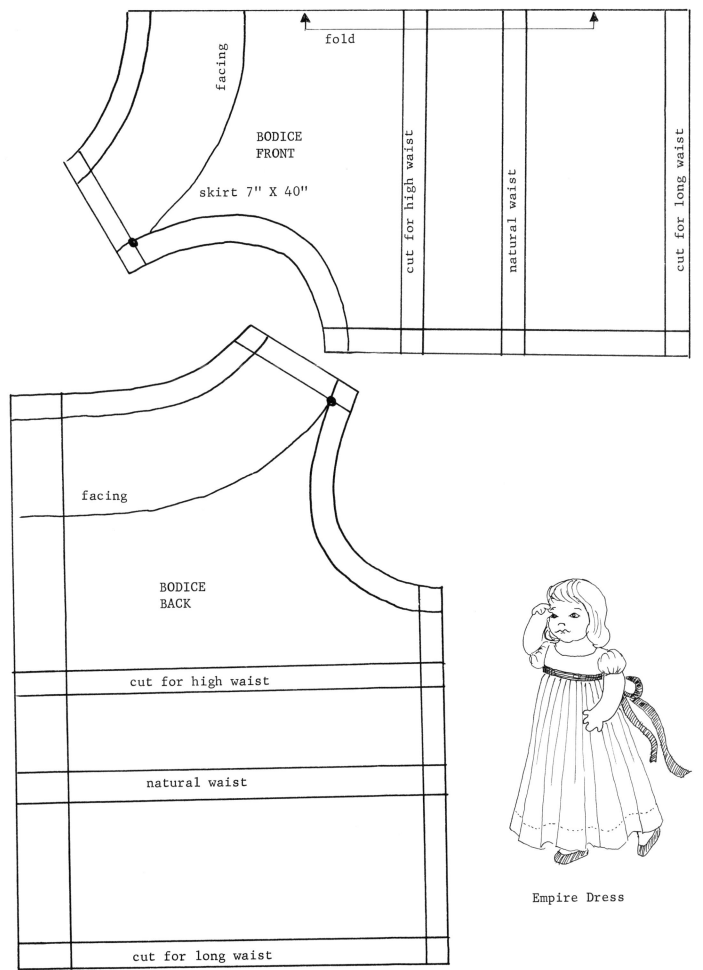

facing

BODICE
FRONT

skirt 7" X 40"

fold

cut for high waist

natural waist

cut for long waist

facing

BODICE
BACK

cut for high waist

natural waist

cut for long waist

Empire Dress

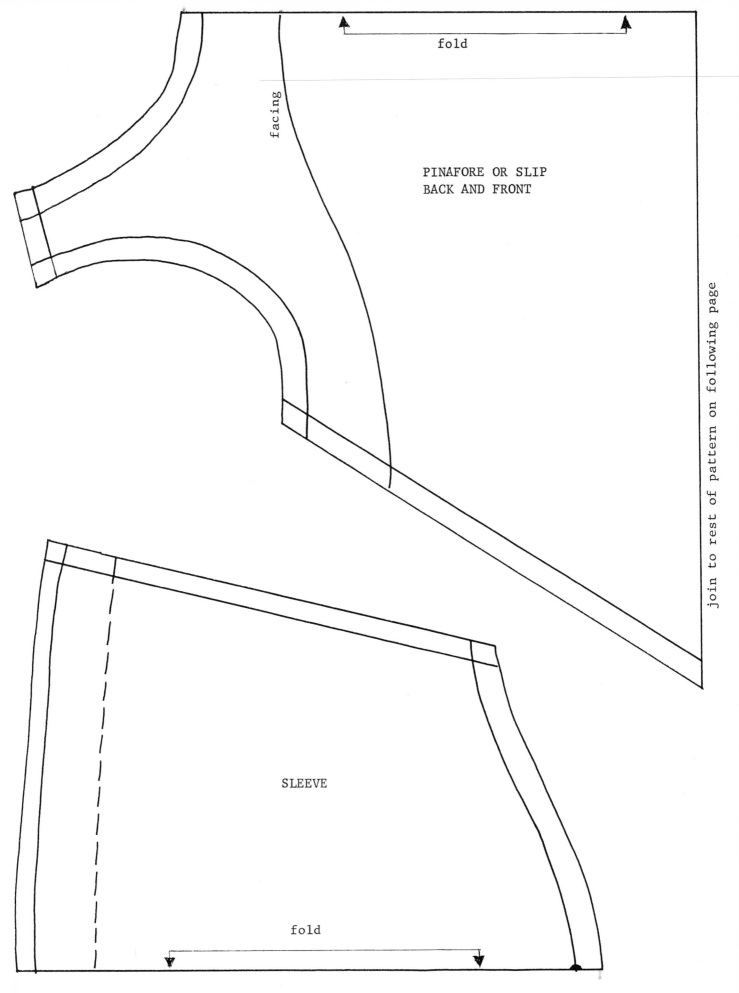

fold

facing

PINAFORE OR SLIP
BACK AND FRONT

join to rest of pattern on following page

SLEEVE

fold

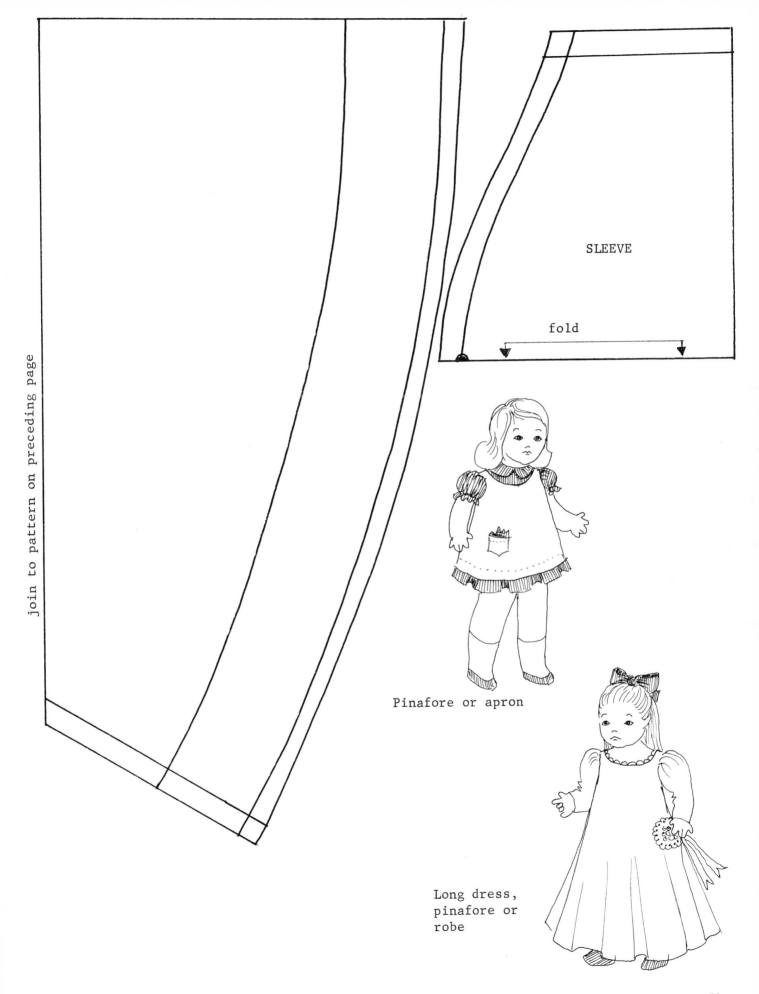

SLEEVE

fold

join to pattern on preceding page

Pinafore or apron

Long dress,
pinafore or
robe

53

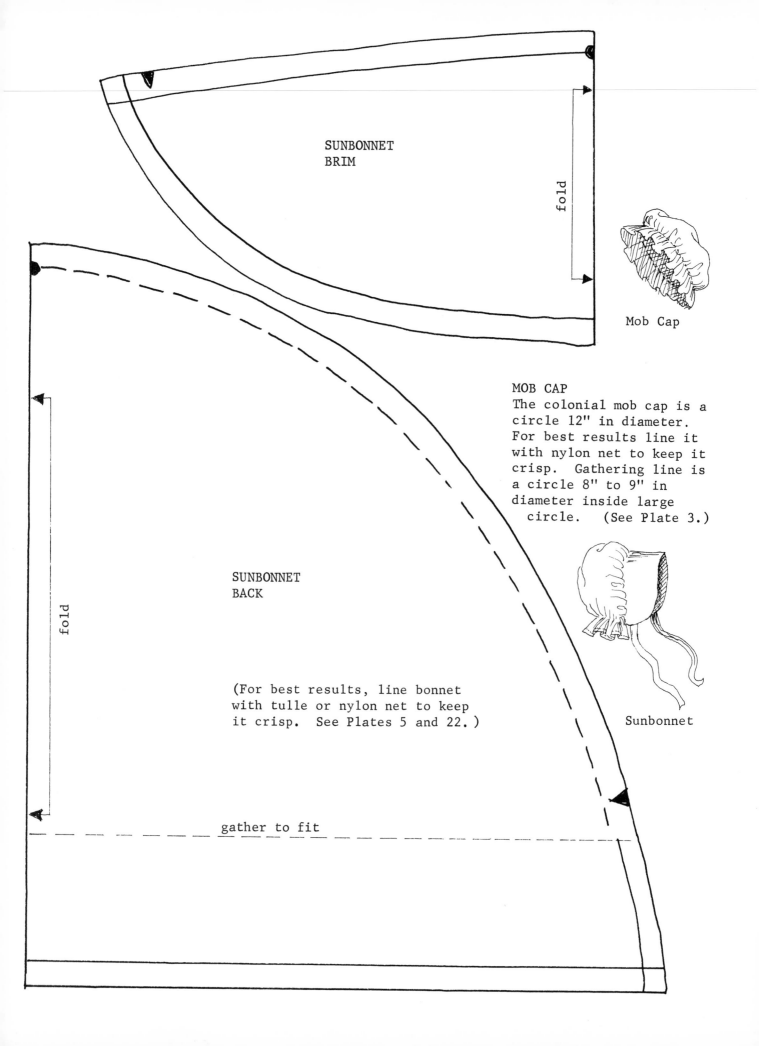

SUNBONNET
BRIM

fold

Mob Cap

MOB CAP
The colonial mob cap is a
circle 12" in diameter.
For best results line it
with nylon net to keep it
crisp. Gathering line is
a circle 8" to 9" in
diameter inside large
 circle.   (See Plate 3.)

SUNBONNET
BACK

(For best results, line bonnet
with tulle or nylon net to keep
it crisp. See Plates 5 and 22.)

Sunbonnet

fold

gather to fit

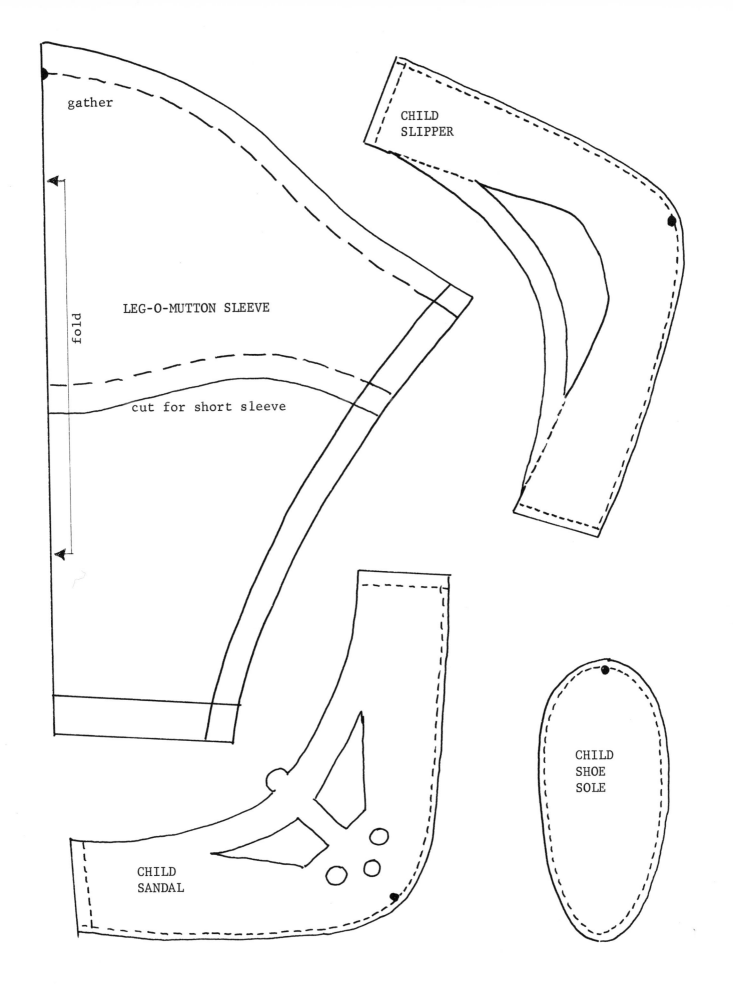

gather

fold

LEG-O-MUTTON SLEEVE

cut for short sleeve

CHILD
SLIPPER

CHILD
SANDAL

CHILD
SHOE
SOLE

55

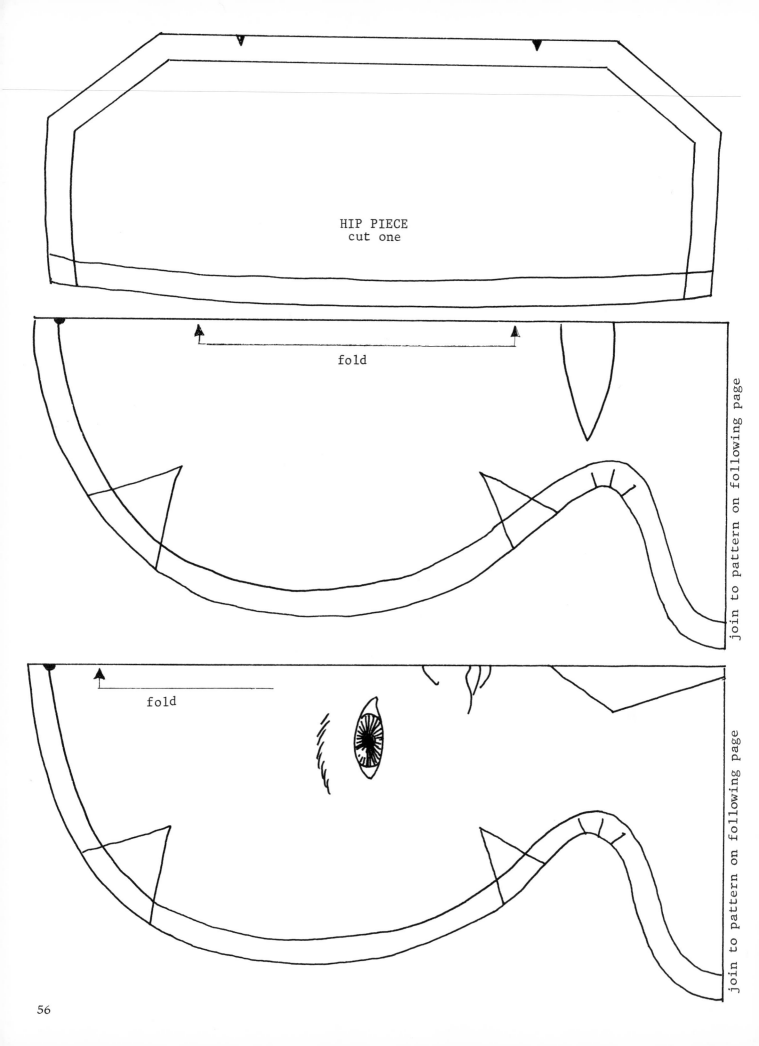

HIP PIECE
cut one

fold

fold

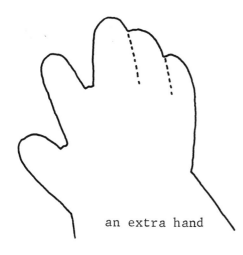

an extra hand

GIRL DOLL

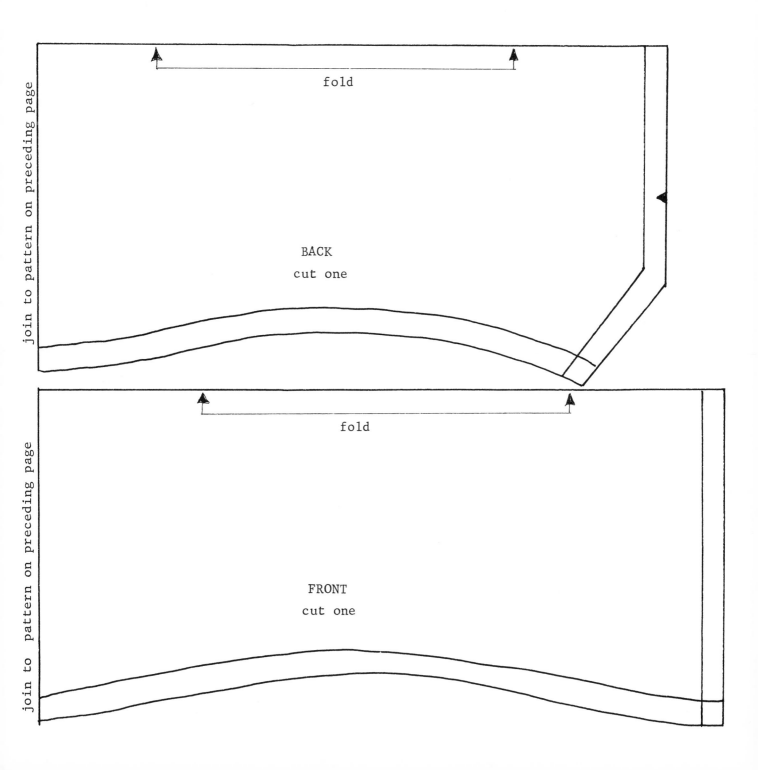

fold

join to pattern on preceding page

BACK
cut one

fold

join to pattern on preceding page

FRONT
cut one

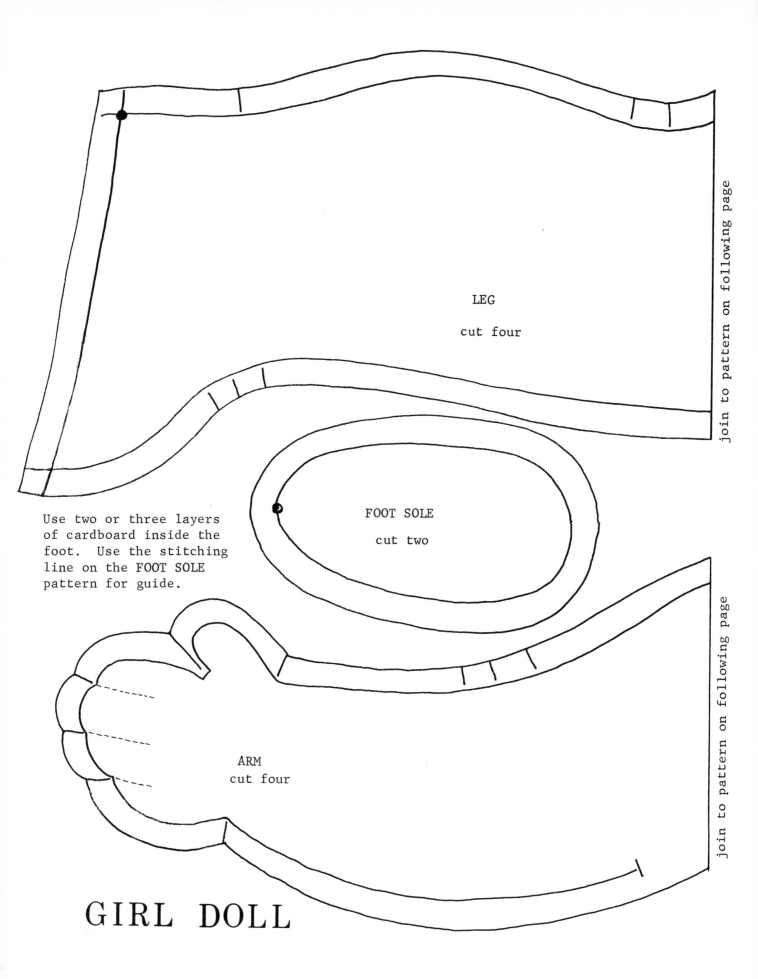

LEG

cut four

FOOT SOLE

cut two

Use two or three layers
of cardboard inside the
foot. Use the stitching
line on the FOOT SOLE
pattern for guide.

ARM
cut four

join to pattern on following page

join to pattern on following page

GIRL DOLL

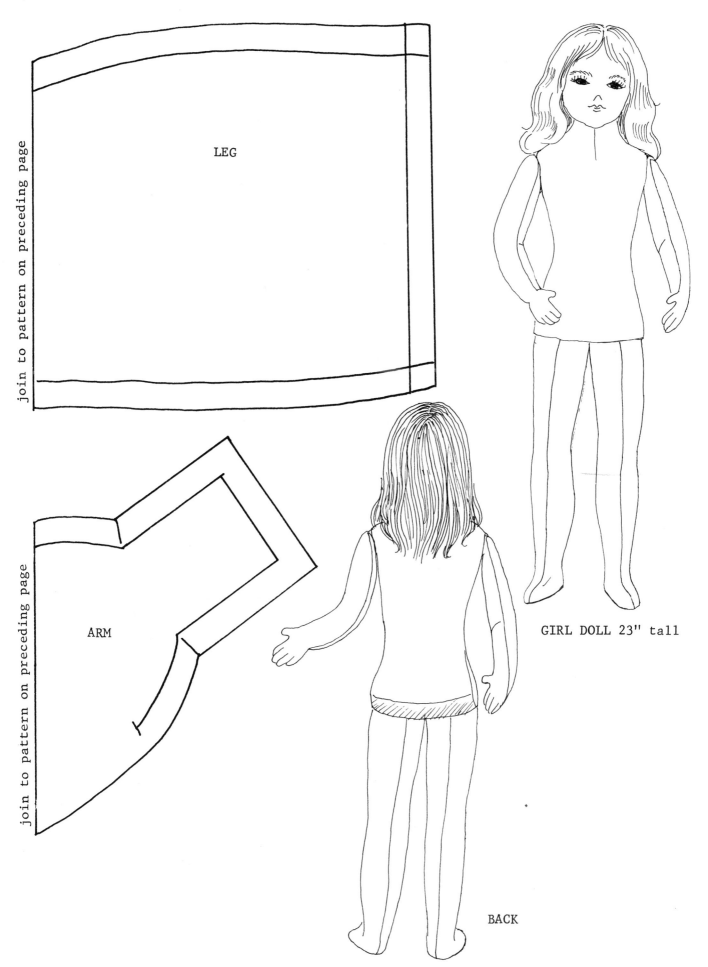

LEG

join to pattern on preceding page

ARM

join to pattern on preceding page

GIRL DOLL 23" tall

BACK

59

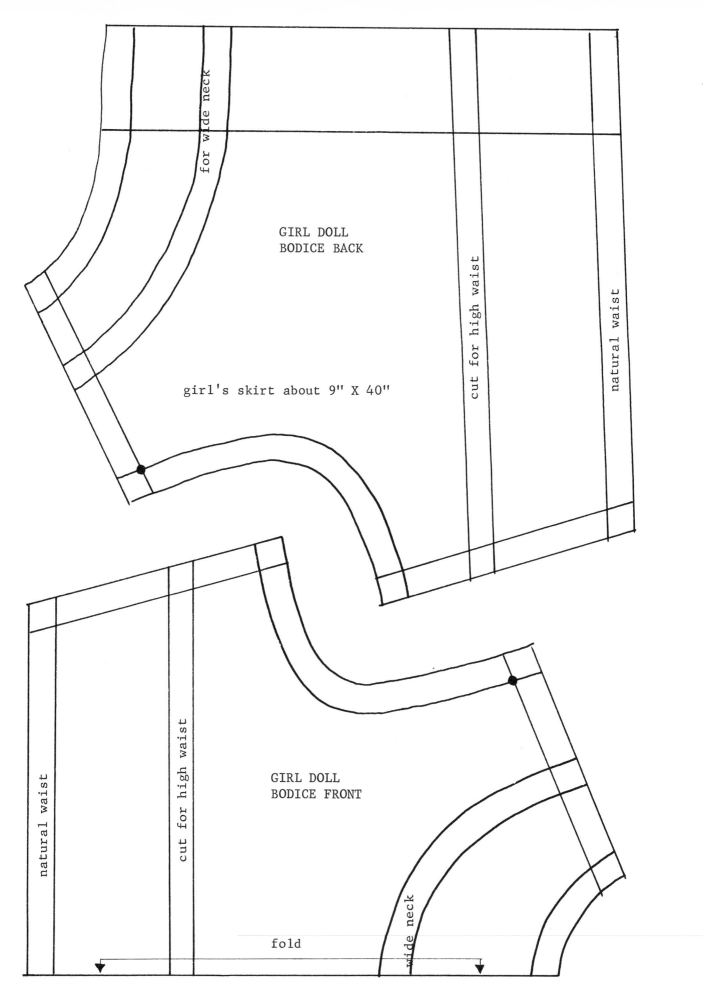

GIRL DOLL
BODICE BACK

girl's skirt about 9" X 40"

for wide neck

cut for high waist

natural waist

natural waist

cut for high waist

GIRL DOLL
BODICE FRONT

wide neck

fold

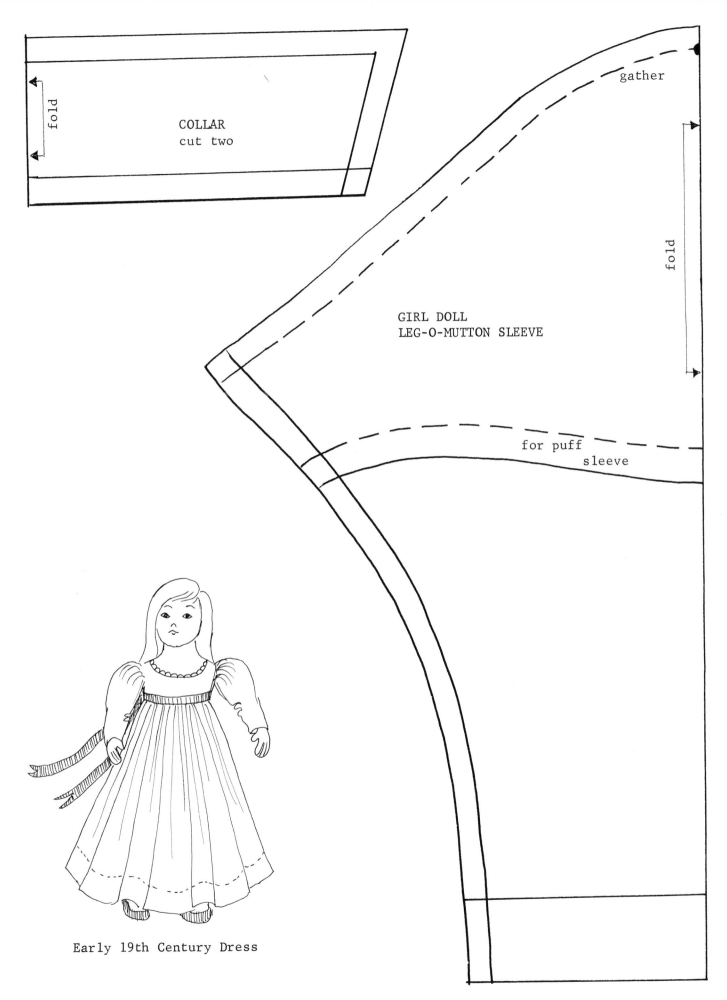

COLLAR
cut two

fold

GIRL DOLL
LEG-O-MUTTON SLEEVE

gather

fold

for puff
sleeve

Early 19th Century Dress

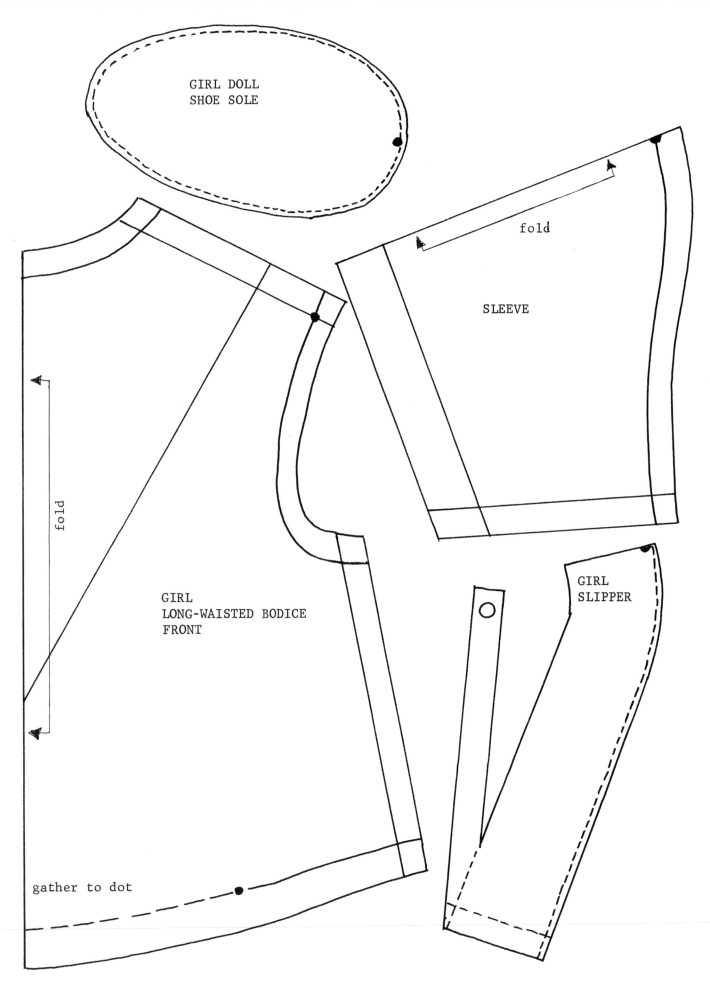

GIRL DOLL
SHOE SOLE

fold

SLEEVE

fold

GIRL
LONG-WAISTED BODICE
FRONT

GIRL
SLIPPER

gather to dot

skirt about 9" X 40"
long skirt 17" X 40"

Old Fashioned or party dress

GIRL
LONG-WAISTED BODICE
BACK

gather to dot

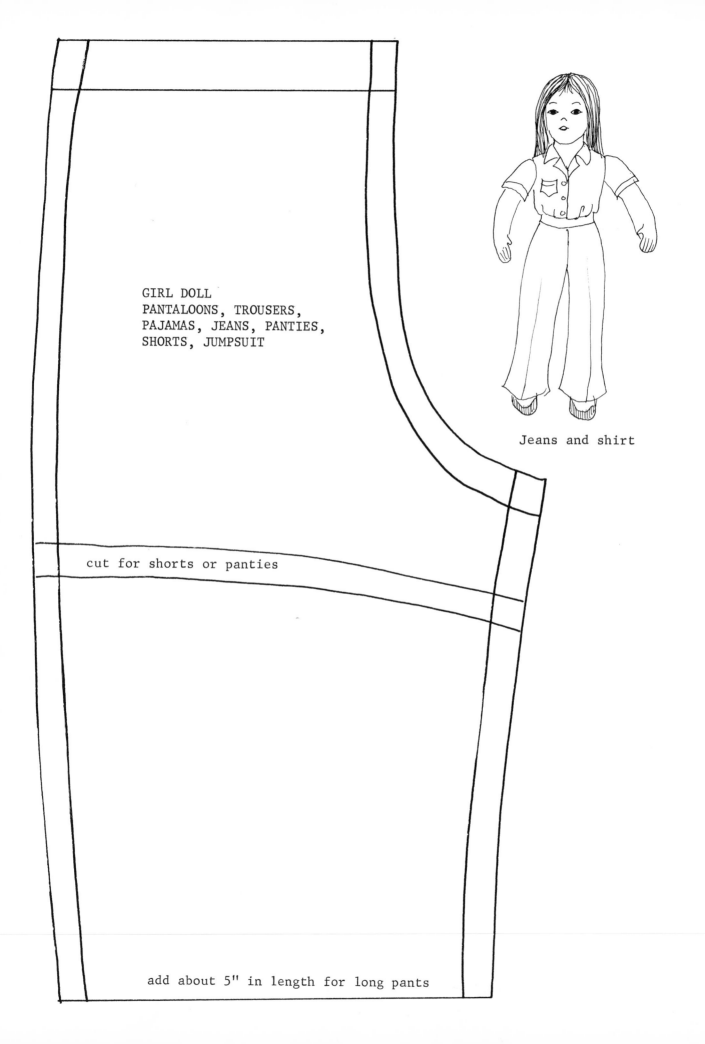

GIRL DOLL
PANTALOONS, TROUSERS,
PAJAMAS, JEANS, PANTIES,
SHORTS, JUMPSUIT

Jeans and shirt

cut for shorts or panties

add about 5" in length for long pants

3. The Dolls' Faces

EMBROIDERED FACES

Using a single thread of either regular sewing thread or embroidery floss, outline the eyes with a small backstitch or outline embroidery stitch. Complete faces are on pattern page 72. On fair-skinned dolls use a medium or dark brown thread, on dark-skinned dolls use black.

Next, with the same color thread work the eyebrows with small individual stitches at an angle. (Plates 26 and 38) If you want to achieve an old-fashioned look, just use the outline stitch for the brows, too, to give a long, thin look like that on antique dolls.

With a blue, green, gray, brown, or very dark brown thread embroider the iris of the eye with a blanket, buttonhole, or eyelet stitch radiating out from a center circle. The blanket stitch should be worked *outward* so that the iris is automatically outlined. If you have examined a real eye up close you will notice that it is made up of radiating bands of color in much the same way! Remember that the iris is partly covered by the eyelids, above and below, and, therefore is more oval than round. Leave space in the corners. When both irises are done, fill in the pupil with a black thread in a satin stitch as in Plates 37 and 38. For dark-skinned dolls add white at the corners of the eyes as in Plates 13 and 25.

The white sparkle or highlight is added over the iris to one side of the pupil, covering just the tiniest bit of one side of the pupil. It can be round, long, or star-shaped. Be sure that it is on the same side on both eyes or the doll will appear cross-eyed. I prefer to put the highlight to the right side, but either side works fine.

Outline the nose in either the same color as the eye outline or the lip color. I usually use the same pink as the lips. I prefer a deep pink, salmon, or coral color but have used orange, red, and even tan. Sometimes real babies' lips are quite red. For black dolls I use tan or bright pink.

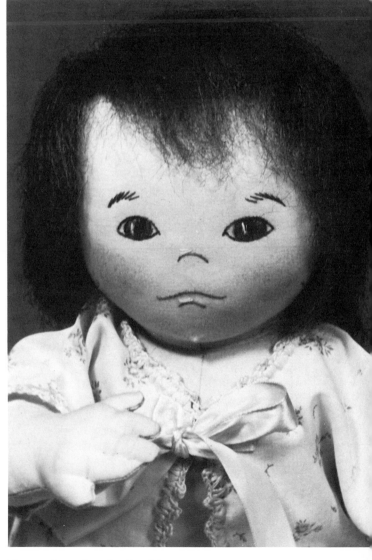

Plate 26. A simple embroidered face.

65

The little white highlights on the nose and lower lip are optional. Sometimes I use them, sometimes I don't. (Plate 26) Just be sure that they are on the same side as the highlights on the eyes. Your light must all come from the same direction. When doing boy dolls' faces I always use the baby and toddler lips instead of the child or girl lips (Plates 24 and 30) no matter which size pattern I use.

It is interesting that the highlights, particularly on the eyes, will not only add sparkle and depth to your doll's face but will make the eyes appear actually to change their direction and expression as you turn the doll. The photographer managed to capture this effect in Plates 36 and 37.

I prefer to draw on the facial features when I cut out the doll but embroider it *after* the doll is stuffed and assembled. Some dollmakers I know prefer to embroider the face with a small hoop before stuffing. I do it after stuffing, mainly, I think, because it is more exciting to see the doll literally come to life in my hands, to take on its personality as I work. I often keep a wig nearby and stop at times to try it on to see how the face will look because I can't wait any longer!

The best rouge I've ever found is a light red or pink colored pencil. It goes on smoothly and stays on. Keep the pencil blunt or rounded, not sharp. It is the only rouge I have ever used which I can control completely; it won't blotch or streak.

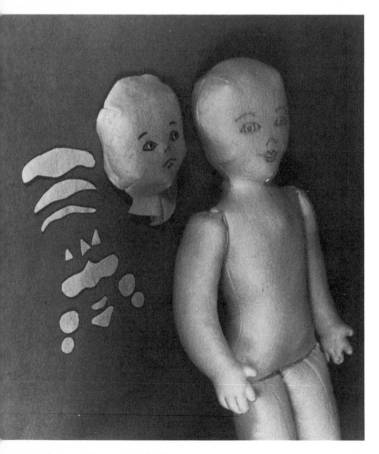

Plate 27. Contouring the face.

The Girl Doll and the Fashion Dolls can have blue or green eyeshadow done with colored pencils also.

With the completing of the face and hair the doll takes on that inevitable personality which all of them acquire! You will find that at times a doll will be determined to take on a certain mischievous, wistful, or pouty look and that the hair or clothes you had planned for it don't look quite right.

In creating puppets, dolls or any people figure, or animal works of art, there is a point when the figure begins to actually participate in its own creation. The personality that emerges may be quite different from the one you were expecting. That's the fun and the excitement of it! We can never be completely sure of the outcome. There is always a bit of mystery there!

You can do the faces with fabric paints of the ball-point or felt tip variety or even with oil paints and brush. The puppedoll toddler in sleepers in Plate 5 has painted features.

CONTOURING THE FACES

Books about dolls put cloth or rag dolls in two categories, those with sewn faces without noses and those with molded faces and noses. Well, a cloth doll *can have a beautiful sewn face with a nose, contoured features, sparkling eyes, and even eyelashes, too!*

My dolls' heads are designed so that the cheek and chin darts make the cheeks puff out and the chin point. The head darts give a well-defined forehead. All this can be accentuated by packing, pressing with your fingers on the eyes and nose bridge, and by lifting the nose and eyebrows up with a large needle or pin. It is surprising how much suggestion of a nose you can achieve by holding your thumb at the bridge of the nose, between the eyes, and pressing. At the same time you do this, go in at the nose, at an angle, with a large needle or pin and lift up. By inserting the needle at the embroidered line of the nose you won't leave holes in the cloth. You can lift and press rather hard, stretching the cloth and lifting the stuffing inside at the same time. You can shape a felt face almost as much as a molded face.

Although I think that my simple embroidered doll faces have charm in their own right, I do occasionally like to make them three-dimensional, to contour them.

You can contour the face on a doll made of cotton percale as is the baby's face in Plates 1 and 29, but contouring works best when making your dolls of felt like that of Plate 28.

First draw the features on your doll front as directed when cutting the doll body. After the doll is complete, make a new face like those on pattern pages 73 or 74. The Toddler and Child Dolls use the same contours as the baby face, even though the heads vary in size. Check the doll patterns for the correct head size for them. This is not a new head, just a new face. Sew the darts in the head, cheeks, and chin as indicated and embroider the features on the new face as in Plate 27.

Next, cut the three graduated sizes of forehead pieces from felt, the large piece for across the cheeks and nose, several circles for each cheek, at least three graduated triangles for the nose and two or three rounded triangles for the chin. You can use as many pieces as you want, depending on how much contouring you desire. Plate 28 shows the completed face.

For best results, *start with your smallest pieces first.* DO NOT GLUE ANYTHING YET. Place the smallest circle on the doll's cheek, then the next largest on top of it and the largest on top of that. Push a pin through all layers to hold them in place. Do the other cheek and then the large nose and cheek piece to cover all these. Notice how you can gently round each piece down over the smaller one under it. The nose pieces should go on top of this large nose and cheek piece. After the forehead and chin contours are pinned in place, you can stretch the embroidered face over it. It works well if you stretch the face a bit at the nose and cheeks first, but be careful not to damage it.

Pull the embroidered face over the contoured face of the doll and pin it all around at the seam. You can tell at this point how your face will look. You can decide if you want more build-up at the nose or cheeks. As long as you haven't glued anything yet, you can experiment. When you are pleased with the way it looks, take the face off and place a bit of glue under each contour shape and remove the pins.

It is at this point that you must decide whether you want the face to stay soft, or to be firm and more controlled. The face can be firm or soft, depending on the amount of glue you use. If you are a purist, just put a few dots of glue on the contour pieces to hold them in place before putting on the embroidered face.

If you want the face to be firm, you can achieve more refinement by gluing the entire face and doing a certain amount of sculpturing, as follows: With a brush put a thin layer of glue over the entire face of the doll and the contours. Let it dry for several minutes until the glue is only slightly sticky. Stretch the embroidered face over the glued, contoured one and pin around the seam as you did above.

For still more contouring, take your fingers and press gently at the eyes and bridge of the nose and at the corners of the mouth under the cheeks. Take a large needle and lift up the nose, eyebrows, and chin. This lifting and pressing will further round out and sculpture the face. Although you can do this as much as you like while the glue is still soft, I personally think that cloth dolls look best when the facial contours are subtle; in other words, I think contouring should remain simple and merely serve to emphasize the embroidered face. When dry, the face will be quite firm and permanent.

When contouring a doll made of cotton-polyester or all cotton percale, such as shown in Plate 29, there is one extra step involved. The embroidered percale face needs a lining underneath it to smooth it out as

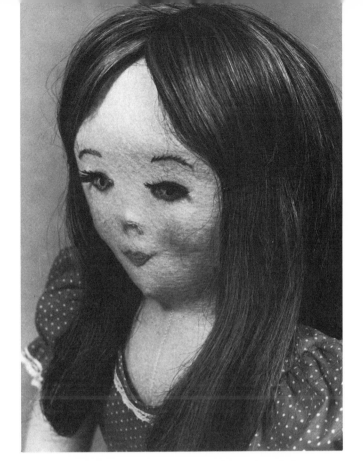

Plate 28. The completed contoured face of felt with eyelashes.

Plate 29. A contoured face of percale with eyelashes.

67

the cloth doesn't have the thickness and softness of felt and reveals too much. I cut and sew *two* faces; one the same cloth as the doll which I embroider, and the other a plain one of felt, cotton flannel, or some other very soft material in a pink or white color. This additional underlining only takes a little extra time since it is not embroidered. It is the underlining that is glued, very lightly, to the face. Use glue only at the eyes of the outer percale face. Just one dot behind each embroidered eye will keep the eye back down in the hollow place for it, rather than have it stretch across.

Other dolls with contoured faces shown are the puppedoll toddler, Happy, in Plate 5, the Baby Shirley in Plate 12, and Kathy, the Child Doll in Plate 22.

NOSES

There is more than one way to create a cloth doll face with three-dimensional noses and features. Plates 2 and 30 show a little boy and Plate 3 shows a blonde child with noses built up on cotton percale faces. The large percale girl doll in blue in Plate 4 also has a percale nose.

This is done by cutting *on the bias* a series of small triangles of the same fabric as the doll's face. Use the contoured nose triangles of pattern pages 73 and 74 plus one slightly larger one. Glue them onto the face, starting with the smallest first and working up to the largest. It might be a good idea to experiment on a padded piece of cloth or even on the back of the doll's head first to see how it works. (You can dampen it and pull it off later, or just let the hair cover it.) Sometimes I use pink or white felt for the underneath layers because it is thicker and then use the percale only as the largest, outer piece. Paint each triangle completely with glue on one side and place it on the face directly above the embroidered nose with the edge of the nose resting on the embroidered line.

The last and largest piece, cut on the bias so it won't ravel, should be glued as flat against the face as possible at the sides and bridge of the nose. Press at the bridge and let it curve slightly at the base so that it rounds out. Don't work with it too much. You can wet your finger and smooth the edges of the cloth.

After the nose has dried, you may want to add a small moon-shaped piece underneath the nose to cover the layered edges. Sometimes it isn't needed, but most often is. It must fit perfectly so keep trimming it while *dry* with your scissors. When it fits, glue it on. Your doll will take on the most unexpected character with a touch of humor when you do this!

The small-scale 17 inch Fashion Dolls of Plates 7, 34, 35, and 52, have three-dimensional embroidered noses. I used a pink thread which perfectly matches the percale of the doll. I used a satin stitch in a triangular shape, working it over and over and building it up. Most of the depth is at the bottom of the nose, graduating to a flat point at the bridge. You can put the tiniest speck

of felt underneath to help build it out. The nose can be lifted up at the tip by inserting a strong needle and pulling the whole nose out and up, while pressing between the eyes.

HARD FACES

The felt toddler in Plate 31 has an embroidered face of felt with a built-up nose. After adding the nose, I painted the face with about five coats of white liquid glue, making it almost like a china face because of the translucent look. Elmer's Glue-all is very good but there are other brands suitable. I buy Witt's glue in bulk (by the quart or half-gallon) at the hardware store for general use. U.S. Gypsum makes one brand called Durabond and the Sloman Co. makes one called Sobo which is recommended by handicraft stores for use on cloth. The term "liquid white glue" will usually bring forth what you are looking for in most stores. (Frankly, once I pour the glue into my glue-pot I couldn't tell you which one I'm using.) When I originally embroidered this doll's face, I felt that I made her nose too high so the day I decided to experiment with the glue I thought, "If it doesn't work, well, I wasn't altogether happy

Plate 30. A built-up nose of cotton percale on a plain face.

Plate 31. A built-up nose on a hard face of felt.

with the face anyway, so why not?" I built up the felt nose and then over a period of several days put on the five thick coats of glue. As dolls have a way of doing, she became one of my favorites, with her little snooty nose and china-doll skin and blonde curls. When dressing the dolls it seemed so natural to have her be the one all dressed up in the coat and hat.

The little tomboy in Plates 21, 32, and 33 has an embroidered, one-hundred-percent-cotton broadcloth face with a built-up nose. She also has several coats of liquid white glue. This method offers many possibilities. As the first coat of glue dries there is a point at which it is not sticky to your fingers but is still pliable in that first hour or so, depending on the humidity where you work. At this point, you can lift the upper lip, chin, cheeks and eyebrows with a needle and press the eyes and corners of the mouth with your fingers. Be sure you are pleased with it before you finish this because it will dry this way and become quite permanent. The following coats of glue will add smoothness. The result looks much like a wax-head doll. Incidentally, you can put a layer of wax over the hard faces, if you like.

Plate 32. A built-up nose on a hard face of cotton cloth.

Plate 33. The hard face of cotton cloth shown in profile.

EYELASHES

The Toddler Doll, designed after my daughter Clare, in Plates 2, 36, and 37 has just a simple embroidered face with real eyelashes as does the Elizabeth doll in Plates 3 and 38. They are the usual cosmetic false eyelashes which come in strip form. There is no need to pay a lot of money for them. If you have a friend who admits wearing them, just ask her to save you her old ones. I have also found that drug and variety stores have cheap eyelashes on sale from time to time for as little as two pairs for a dollar!

Since the eyelash strip is for human eyes, it must be measured to fit the doll's eye. It should go from the outside corner to about ⅛ to ¼ inch short of the inside corner. (There are eyelashes called minilashes or demilashes, which are short strips for only the outside corners of a woman's eyes. These are just the right size for dolls.) I save the short strip I cut off to use on small dolls, such as those in Plates 34 and 39.

To attach the eyelash take a toothpick or pin and put a line of glue onto the strip, holding the lashes. Then, still using the toothpick, make a thin line of glue on the doll just above the embroidered eyelid, barely touching it. Let this dry for a minute or two and then put the lash in place, using the clean end of the toothpick to press it into place. Do the other eye.

It is most important that you place the lashes in as natural a position as possible, more out than up. They will dry in this position. After they are dry and the glue feels hard, you should go back and reinforce them with more glue, making sure they are well adhered. Let just a little glue go over the strip between the individual hairs, locking the strip in place.

Eyelashes come in many sizes. Those on Clare and Elizabeth are just as I bought them. Those on the baby in Plates 1 and 29, both dolls in Plates 4, and the puppedoll child in the bonnet in Plate 5 all have lashes which had to be trimmed with scissors because they were too long for the dolls. They were trimmed after the glue was quite dry.

The lashes of the Fashion Dolls in Plates 34 and 39 had to be trimmed quite short. Oh yes, Mabear has eyelashes, too! (Plate 6)

in Plates 1 and 29, both dolls in Plate 4, and the puppe-toured and she has eyelashes as well. The girl doll of Plates 4 and 28 also has both contouring and eyelashes.

Plate 34. A built-up thread nose and tiny eyelashes on the small scale Fashion Doll.

Plate 35. A built-up thread nose, and hair wig on a small scale Fashion Doll.

Plate 36. The embroidered highlights make the eye appear to look one way one moment . . .

Plate 37. . . . and another direction the next moment. The eyelashes are untrimmed.

Plate 38. The exaggerated eyelashes are untrimmed because they are part of the character of this doll.

Plate 39. An embroidered face, tiny eyelashes and embroidery floss hair on a small scale Fashion Doll.

FACES

TODDLER DOLL

BABY DOLL

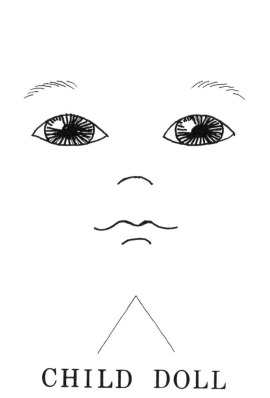

CHILD DOLL

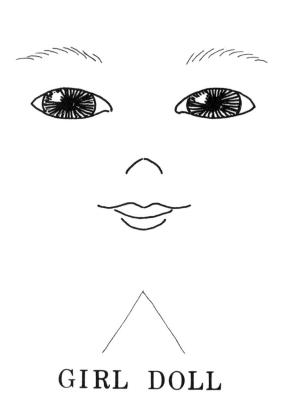

GIRL DOLL

CONTOURING THE FACES

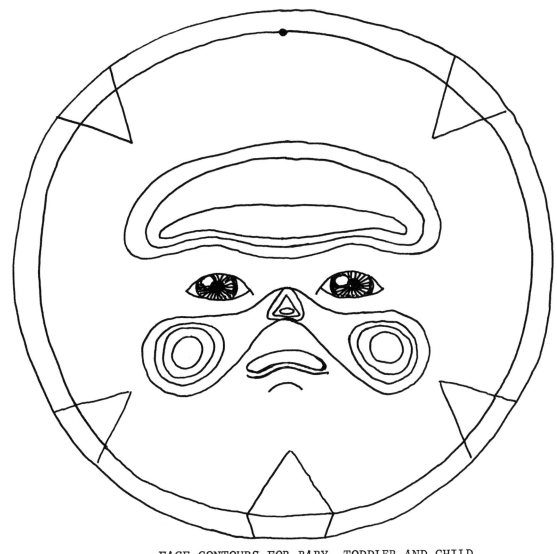

FACE CONTOURS FOR BABY, TODDLER AND CHILD

FACE CONTOURS FOR GIRL DOLL

4. The Dolls' Hair

THE FUR CLOTH WIG CAP

Using the pattern on page 77, cut a rectangle of fur cloth 10 by 4½ inches as in step **a.** Pin the wig pattern to it as shown in Plate 40.

It is a good idea to check the pile to see which way the hairs naturally go. Turn your pattern so that the hairs go *toward the front* of the wig.

Cut from the back side of the fur cloth, cutting just the backing, not the hairs. Whether using real fur or fur cloth, it is the same method. After the piece is cut, give it a good brushing with a hair brush.

From the back side whip-stitch all four darts around the face and neck as in steps **b** and **c.** Whipping keeps the wig cap flat and does not catch the hairs. Try the wig on the doll, pinning it tightly in place. If it comes together neatly in the center back then take it off and whip the back seam from the inside as in step **d.** (If it is too large it can be trimmed so that it just comes together.) Leave the little curved crown piece unsewn as in step **e** until the wig cap is sewn or glued to the doll's head. The hair can be parted on either side as in step **f** or in the middle. If it is short fur, it can just be brushed toward the face all around. You can cut the top hair in bangs or pin it back with a bobby pin, bent in a curve to fit the head, or a clip.

Pin the wig to the head by pulling it down and towards the face and forcing it snugly on the head; pin in place. When you are sure you have it like you want it, sew or glue it to the head all around the face and neck.

After a good brushing, sew or glue the crown piece down over the top edge of the back. When it is brushed the crown hair will blend in with the back hair, making an invisible seam. With practice this whole wig can be done so skillfully that the hair will appear to grow right from the head. (Plates 33, 41, 42, and 43)

Sometimes when I am making more than one doll I embroider the faces and then make the wigs. This way I can try different wigs on the dolls. About one-quarter of the time I use a wig, other than the one originally intended when I visualized the doll. The wig can change the doll's personality.

HAIR WIGS

When using a wig of synthetic or human hair made for humans, take it apart so that you have a very long strip of the sewn hair. Wig shops often have out-of-style wigs on sale for a few dollars. Watch your newspaper for sale advertisements or ask a shop owner to notify you of specials. By the same pattern make a felt or cloth wig cap the same color as the hair as in step **a.** Start sewing the hair strip at the center back at the neck and go all the way around. Sew it right on the edge of the wig cap as in step **b.** When you get back to where you started, begin to spiral it around and around the cap, each row about ½ inch above the last, as in step **c.** It is important to work *up* the cap toward the crown because each row of hair is over the one below as you work.

You can sew a double strip of hair down the center of the head or to one side to make a finished looking part, as in step **d.**

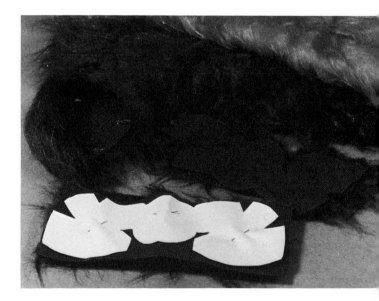

Plate 40. The wig cap pattern, a cut wig cap (center) and a completed wig cap (left). In the rear, yellow and brown fur cloth.

The dark-haired baby in Plate 1, the girl in blue in Plates 4 and 9, the puppedoll toddler in Plate 5, and the toddler doll in Plate 31 all have wigs made in this manner as does the fashion doll in Plate 52. The rows must be closer together on the small-scaled dolls but the method is the same. You can get three doll wigs from a woman's wig with enough left over for one or two miniature dolls.

The toddler Clare in Plates 2 and 9 and the girl in red in Plate 4 have human hair wigs.

Drapery or upholstery fringe can be used in this spiralling manner for doll's hair. It is particularly appropriate for humorous or character dolls because it often appears comic.

EMBROIDERY FLOSS HAIR

Unwind the small floss skeins and rewind them around a heavy cardboard or wood piece 8 inches long. Use from 12 to 16 skeins of floss, depending on how thick you want the hair. See pattern, page 78, step 1.

When you cut the wrapped hair and open it out it will be approximately 16 inches long. Cut a strip of cloth, either the color of the doll's head or the hair, about 5 inches long by 1 inch wide, step 2.

Lay the center of the floss hair across the strip of cloth and sew across it with the smallest stitch on your sewing machine, then turn and go back over it once or twice. Be sure you arrange the hair evenly. as in step 3. You can sew it thicker at one end of the strip so that the front and top hair will be thicker. If you want a side part, you should sew the hair to the strip about 1 inch to one side of the center.

When the hair (floss) is sewn securely, hold one half of the hair firmly and brush the other half with a hair brush to separate the floss into individual strands. Floss is six strands twisted together. Brush the other half. After brushing, the hair can then be combed.

Lay the strip of hair across your doll's head from front to back, pin it in place, and practice some of the suggested hair styles, step 4. (Plates 5, 9, 22, 38, and 39)

When you have decided how you want it, glue the cloth strip to the head and pin in place so that it won't slide as you continue to work. Comb and arrange the hair, then lift it, a section at a time, and put glue on the doll's head as in step 5. Press the hair gently in place, then lift the next section, working toward the back.

I have found only one way to hold the doll steady at the correct level while using both my hands and that is to clutch it between my knees. I can hold up a part

of the hair with one hand, paint a bit of glue on the section of head with the other and then arrange it back in place neatly and accurately this way without having the doll fall over at just the wrong time.

Step 6 shows two long, narrow hair strips put on under the center part strip. They are pulled back and tied with a ribbon. The blonde doll of Plate 3 has this style, mostly hidden by her mob cap. Hers is inexpensive vinyl hair from a costume shop that I cut off a face mask. The dark-skinned doll of Plate 25 has shiny black hair from another similar costume mask.

Step 7 shows straight bangs which are a wide strip of hair under the center part wig. The bangs in step 8 are just wispy little bangs made by tying a few strands together and putting them on with a dot of glue. This can be done on a center or side part. (Plate 38)

A ponytail must be made from a very long strip of rather long hair, long enough to go all the way around the head. It can also be made from a large skein tied in the center and cut as shown in step 9. Lay the hair on the head and arrange it evenly all the way around. Sew or glue in place. When dry, pull it back into the ponytail. This same method was used for the Gibson Girl hair style on the woman in Plates 7 and 34.

Two strips of long hair are put on, one going across the other, for the pulled-back style of step 10. The underneath hair also covers the back of the head. This can be done so that the hair is pulled back from all around the face or just a bit at the center. It can be separated to form two sides similar to step 6.

Use the center part style for braids or side ponytails.

Curls can be made by rolling sections of the hair and sewing or tying each curl in place. The fashion doll child of Plate 7 has embroidery floss curls. Little curls can be looped and sewn in place around the face as on the fashion doll of Plates 7 and 34.

A whole section on authentic period hair styles can be found in my book *The Doll Book* (Van Nostrand Reinhold, 1966) with directions for creating them.

There are various other threads which can be used such as fine crochet thread, and darning and sewing thread which come on large spools. You have to do quite a bit of winding to get enough hair but it is less expensive than embroidery floss. It does not come in the wide range of colors that the floss does but it can be dyed in any color.

The directions for wool or synthetic yarn are much the same as for the floss. The finer yarns are more accurately scaled to the dolls than the heavy ones.

THE WIG CAP

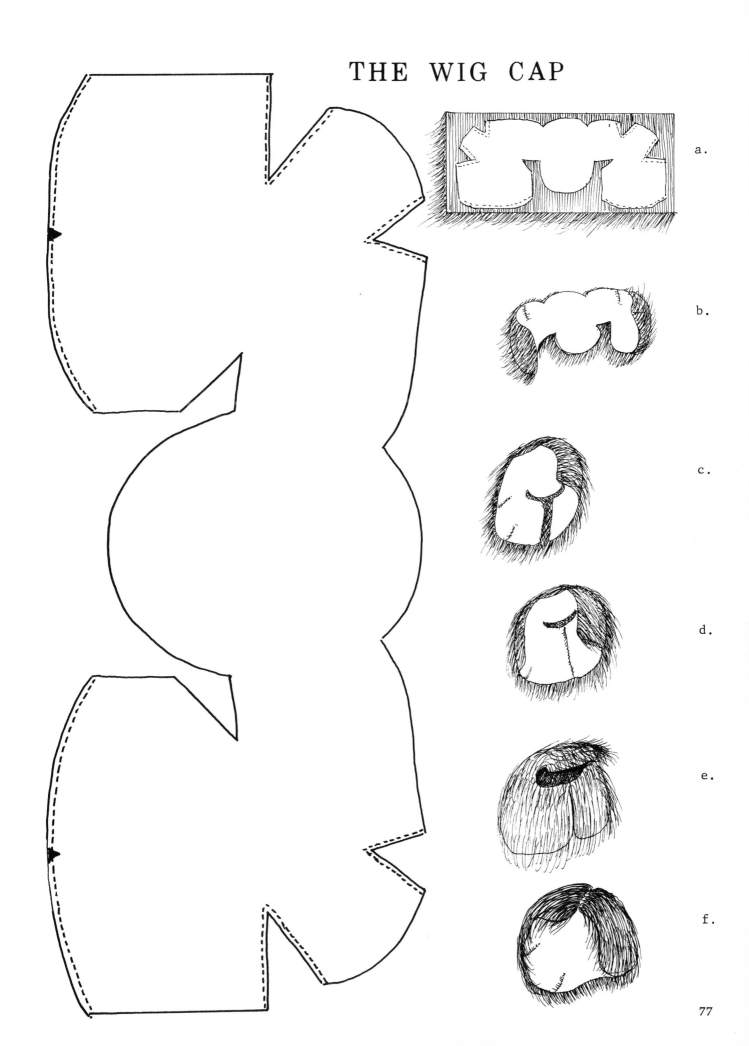

a.

b.

c.

d.

e.

f.

A HAIR WIG

a.

b.

c.

d.

e.

EMBROIDERY FLOSS HAIR

1.

<- 8" ->

2.

3.

5.

4.

6.

8.

7.

9.

10.

5. Puppedolls™

The words doll and puppet have the same origin. The Latin word, *pupa*, meaning girl, was first used for doll because dolls were, "a girl's toy baby." The French use the word *poupée* while the Germans use *puppe* for doll.

There was a time in history when there was only the one art form and only the one word to describe both the puppet and the doll. As the centuries passed, the two became more and more separated until they were looked upon as two different art forms and, of course, two different names for them developed. The word *doll* was not used until the end of the seventeenth century in England.

Doll, it is believed, was short for Dorothy. Apparently a clever street vendor, who had named his dolls after his Dorothy cried out, "Buy my Dolls, Buy my Dolls" and the name stuck!

Adults seem to accept dolls and puppets as two unique forms and to react to each accordingly, but children, especially younger ones, haven't found it so simple.

I have designed both dolls and puppets and written books about both so I have an unprejudiced view of each. Both my dolls and puppets have appeared on national television several times.* Perhaps it's because my family and I are so much at ease with both art forms that the two could come together (again) so naturally in our minds, and in our home.

THE PUPPEDOLL AS PUPPET

A puppet is an object, a human- or animal-like creature which is given life only by a real human being. (If its movement comes from any other source it is not a puppet.) My puppedolls qualify as *real puppets*—but as puppeteer Bill Baird says, "Without a puppeteer, a puppet is lifeless." Not so with my puppedolls! They are never lifeless or limp. Their full, soft bodies remain lifelike and beautiful even after the puppeteer's hand has been removed.

For professional puppet performances there is no substitute for the empty body of a hand puppet. A well-designed puppet is capable, with a good puppeteer, of almost limitless creative expression.

*My dolls have appeared with me on "Today" twice and "Dinah's Place" once. My puppets have appeared with me on "Today" once and on "Dinah's Place" once, without me. Dinah used my "Minnie Pearl" puppet on her show once when the real Minnie was a guest.

But, the puppet as a toy, hobby, creative outlet, or even therapy is a different story altogether and that is exactly where the puppedoll excels! The puppedoll, too, can be an excellent performer in the hands of a pro but its main charm is on a more personal level.

One must always give so much to a puppet, both physically and intellectually, in order to receive from him. Sometimes you would just like to relax and cuddle one; to dress and undress it; and arrange it in different positions. I've seen my own young children, and others, express a sense of frustration upon removing a puppet from a small hand and then, while holding it by its head, try to hug it, make it sit, stand or walk, without success.

I've seen children in bed asleep, hugging a head and hands, attached to a limp body in a heap trying, with little success, to cuddle an empty puppet. It seemed to me a rather touching sight. Most attachments for puppets are short-lived for this reason as the child's affection is shifted to a more responsive doll, Teddy bear, or security blanket.

The puppet, because of its natural appeal, invites us to be his friend and then, having succeeded in winning us over, refuses to allow that friendship to develop.

THE PUPPEDOLL AS DOLL

The puppedoll certainly qualifies as a real doll in every sense of the word; a lovable toy and a thing of beauty and character, able to convey a message to the beholder. Dolls have never really needed justification though—just being a doll is enough. A puppedoll is a doll and more and enjoys the best of two worlds—that of the doll as well as the puppet—and I should add here, a third world, too—that of the cuddly Teddy bear or soft toy animal. No soft toy animal was ever a bit more huggable!

A puppedoll can do many things that dolls can't do and that includes mechanical dolls, too. True, a mechanical doll can "give" but in such a limited way. You wind it up or turn it on and it performs some simple act over and over again or speaks a few words or short sentences over and over again. There is no give-and-take involved and it certainly inspires no *creativity* on the part of the owner as the puppedoll does.

The puppedoll and child relationship will not necessarily be on the same level as that of the collector and his unique doll. The craftsman and his or her creation, in the form of the puppedoll, is a relationship on still another plane. Judging from the reaction of people of all ages who have purchased my puppedolls during the last three years, their attitudes seem to run the gamut from, "I'll give nothing; make no effort, just take from you by enjoying you," to "How much life can I give to you in order to receive from you?"

Not only does the puppet have only as much life as the puppeteer is capable of giving it, but the duration of that life depends on how long the manipulator is willing to give it. The puppet-puppeteer relationship is an all-or-nothing relationship. In contrast, when one has finished manipulating my puppedoll the instinct is to give it a hug, carefully arrange it in a charming position, and then allow it to give to you in the way that only a doll is capable of giving.

THE PUPPEDOLL IN THERAPY

Since the early 1950s, I have advocated using puppets for work with people with physical, emotional, mental, and economic handicaps. I have held puppetry workshops for teachers, medical personnel, and volunteer workers in the Midwest and South for the past twenty years; and in many cases, worked directly with the students or patients. I know the value and still unrealized potential of the puppet in therapy. A puppedoll of one's own can fill an important need for these groups long after the puppet performance is over. My puppedolls may very well find a place in serious therapy someday, but for now they are just for our enjoyment.

Plate 42. The human hand inside the back panel as seen from the rear . . .

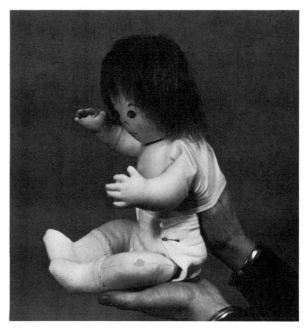

Plate 43. . . . the side . . .

Plate 44. . . . and the front.

Plate 41. The Puppedoll Baby showing the back panel.

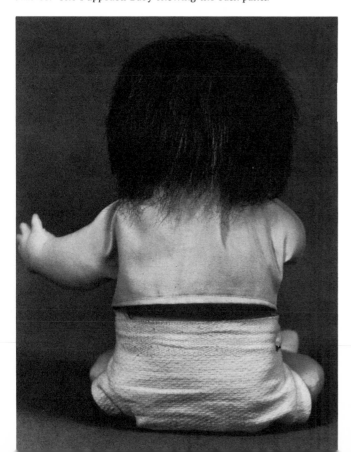

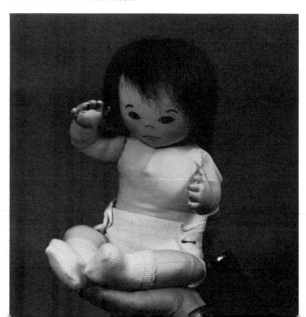

6. Constructing the Puppedoll™

Just what is it that makes a Puppedoll a doll, but more than a doll, while at the same time a puppet, yet more than a puppet? A secret, unique back panel incorporated into the doll's body at the time the doll is assembled gives the puppedoll its "double life." The panel allows it to be both puppet and complete doll at the same time. A Baby Doll with the back puppet panel is shown in Plates 41 through 44.

BABY PUPPEDOLL

The Baby and the Little Baby Puppedolls use the doll bodies, as they are, with only the addition of the puppet panel because the baby dolls already have the arms and body all-in-one which is necessary for Puppedolls.

TODDLER PUPPEDOLL

Since the Puppedoll must fit a human hand, it must, like a puppet, be somewhat shortened through the shoulder and arms while all in one piece. For this reason the Toddler Puppedoll has a body and arms different from those of the Toddler doll. Use the regular Toddler leg pattern with the Toddler puppedoll pattern. A Little Toddler Puppedoll can be made by using the Little Baby pattern in the same manner.

CHILD PUPPEDOLL

This and the Toddler Puppedoll use the same Puppedoll pattern. The instructions indicate where to cut the body for each doll. Since the successful hand puppet is always limited in size to the human hand, the Child Puppedoll has shorter arms than the child doll, just as the Toddler Puppedoll has slightly shorter arms than the Toddler Doll.

When making puppedoll clothes, I usually fold under a bit less of the cloth at the bodice, shirt, or coat openings than on the doll's clothes so that the clothes are sufficiently loose for my hand. No other modifications are necessary. All you need do is try the garment on the doll for a fitting, with your hand in the back panel and set your fasteners where they fit naturally—just as you would fit a person. Sometimes I use ties instead of buttons or snaps because they can always be adjusted to fit. I have used elastic at the waistlines of dresses when I wanted them to fit snugly.

Since the Toddler and Child Puppedolls have shorter arms than the dolls, you will need to shorten the long sleeves to fit them.

The overalls and pajamas and other back-opening clothes are no problem at all. The blue sleepers on the Toddler Puppedoll in Plate 5 have elastic across the back bottoms, making a drop-seat. The puppeteer's hand simply goes in under the pajama top! For the overalls, one's hand is just worked in under the crossed straps and up under the shirt. For dresses, you can either put your hand through the back opening or preferably all the way up under the skirt. Dresses, coats, and pinafores conceal one's hand completely. Only the christening dress and other full-length gowns and dresses require that your hand go in through the back opening instead of under the dress. Actually, you will find only very minor alterations, if any, are necessary when adapting the doll clothes to the puppedoll.

Since the back panel is a permanent part of the puppedoll, rather than an addition to a doll, it is an important part of its construction.

PUPPEDOLL™ BABY

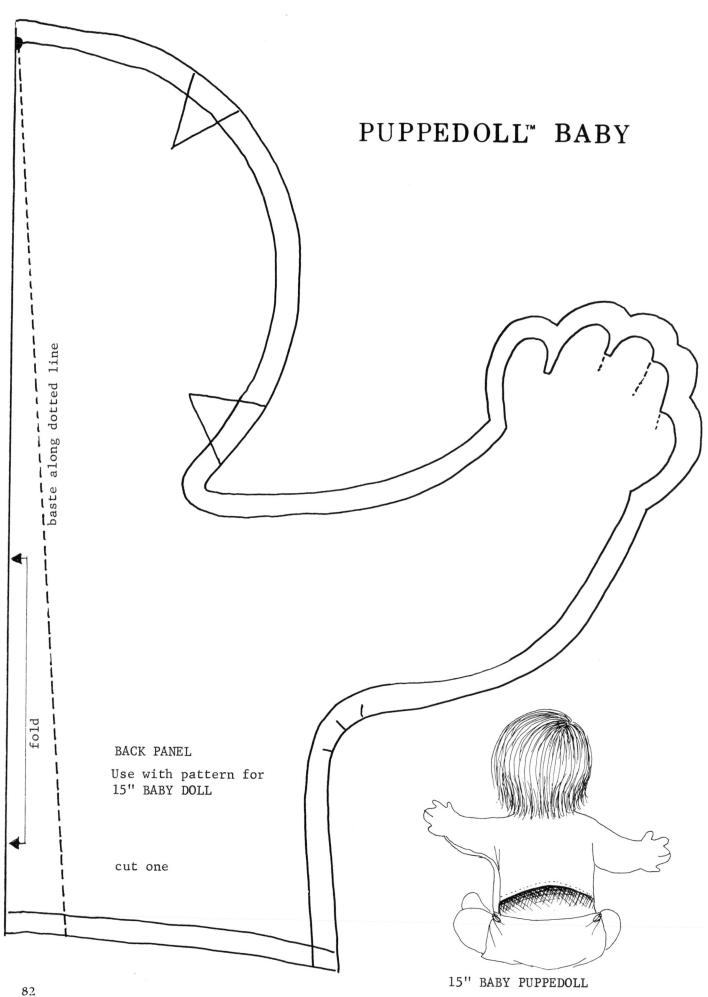

baste along dotted line

fold

BACK PANEL

Use with pattern for
15" BABY DOLL

cut one

15" BABY PUPPEDOLL

82

PUPPEDOLL™
LITTLE BABY

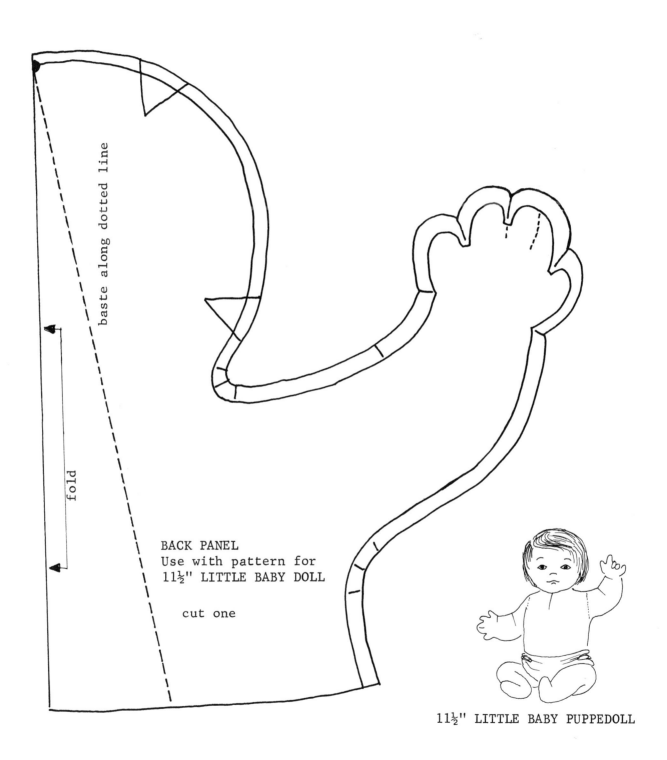

baste along dotted line

fold

BACK PANEL
Use with pattern for
11½" LITTLE BABY DOLL

cut one

11½" LITTLE BABY PUPPEDOLL

PUPPEDOLL™ TODDLER AND CHILD

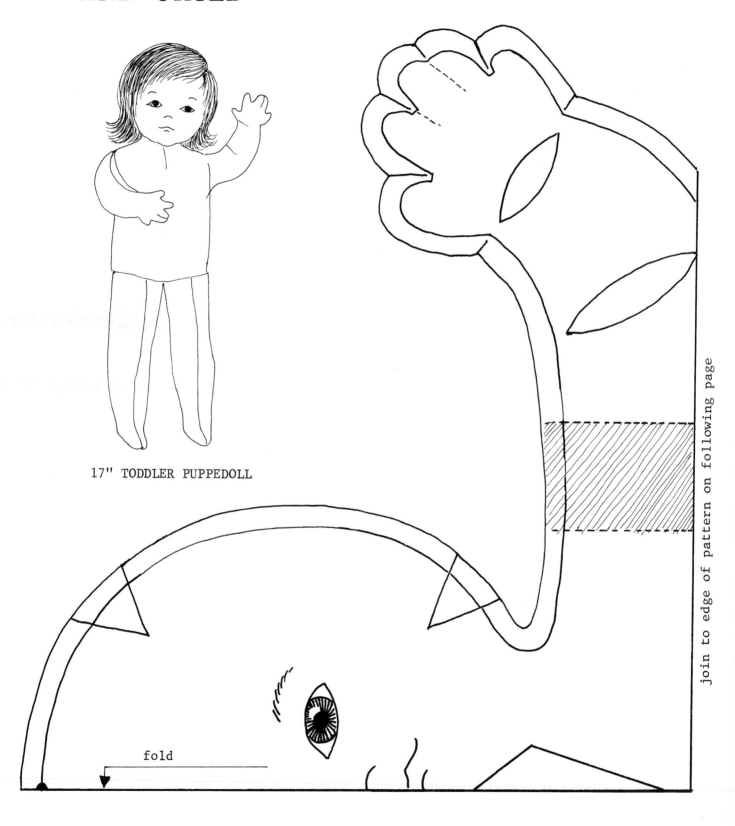

17" TODDLER PUPPEDOLL

fold

join to edge of pattern on following page

Use this PUPPEDOLL body
and back panel with the
TODDLER DOLL and CHILD
DOLL leg patterns

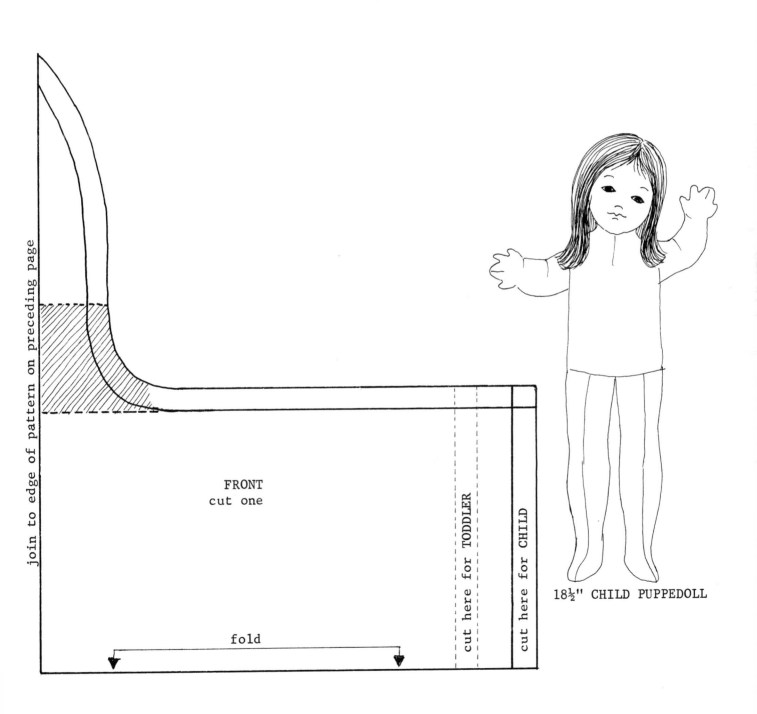

join to edge of pattern on preceding page

FRONT
cut one

cut here for TODDLER

cut here for CHILD

fold

18½" CHILD PUPPEDOLL

PUPPEDOLL™ TODDLER AND CHILD

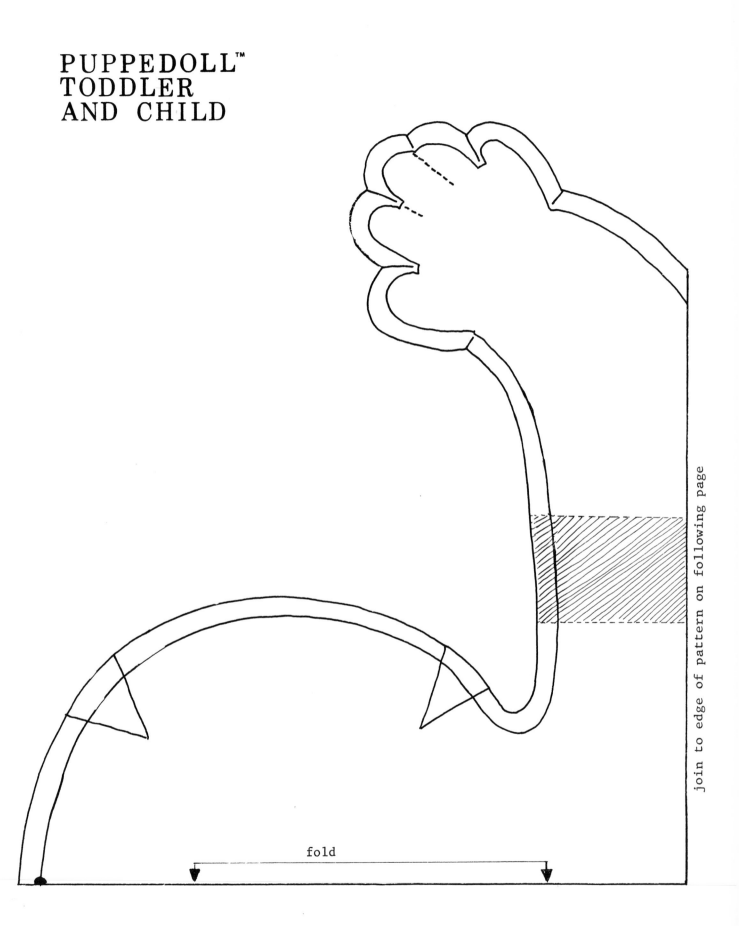

fold

join to edge of pattern on following page

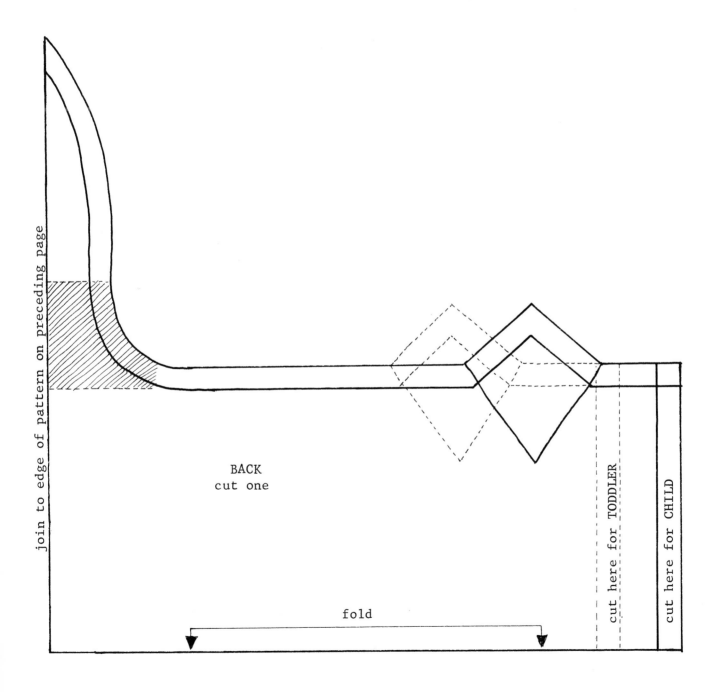

join to edge of pattern on preceding page

BACK
cut one

fold

cut here for TODDLER

cut here for CHILD

PUPPEDOLL™ TODDLER AND CHILD

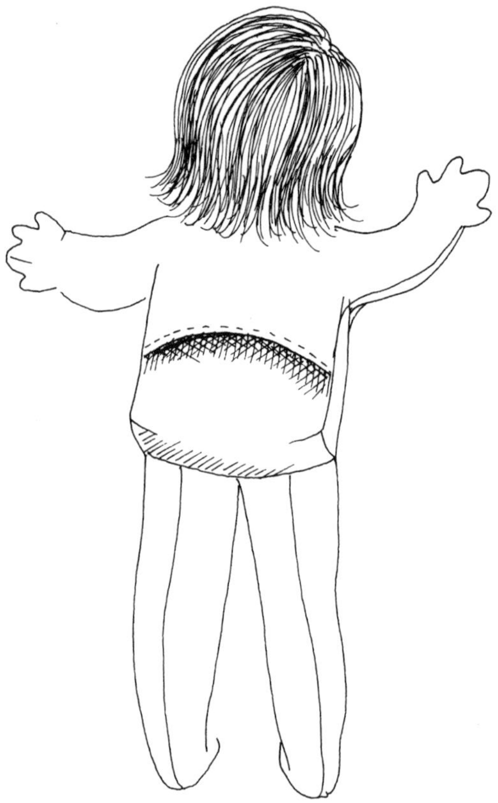

17" TODDLER PUPPEDOLL BACK

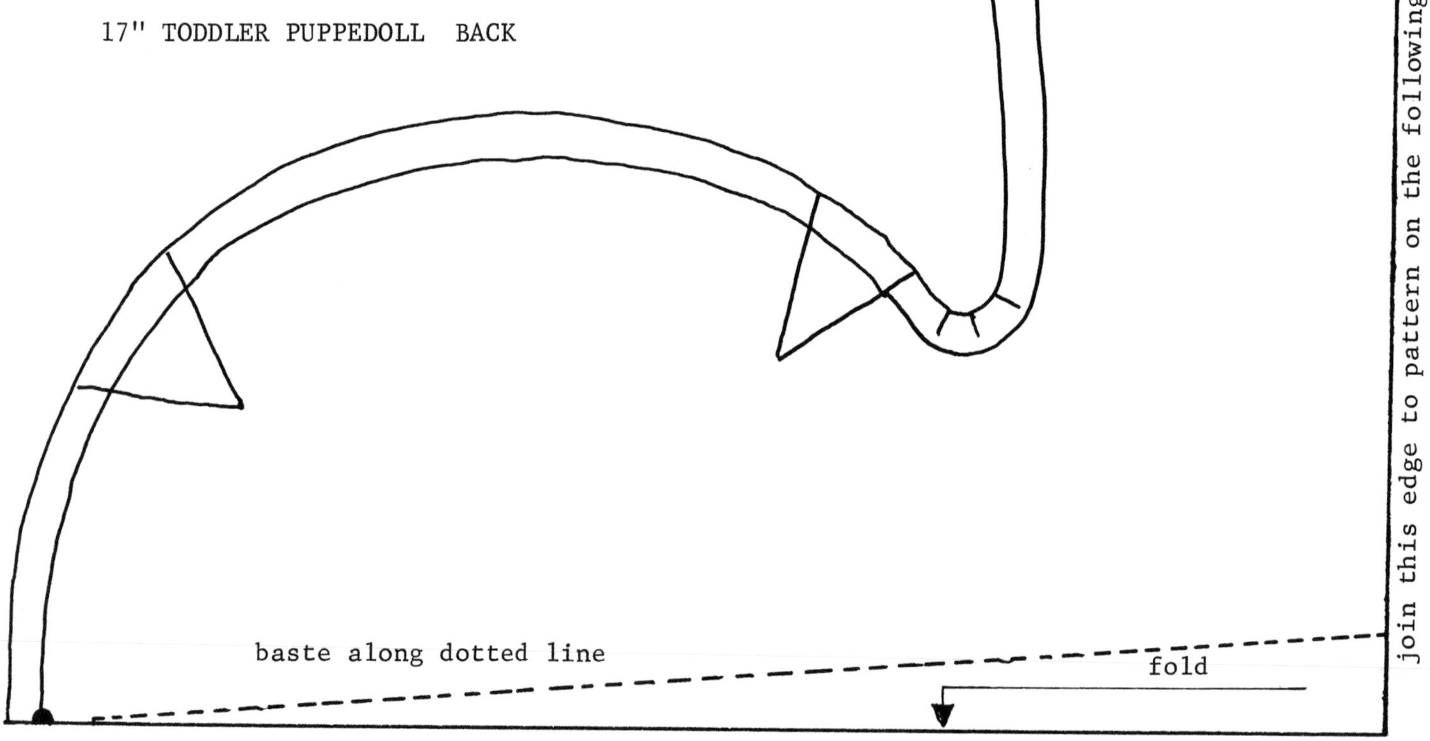

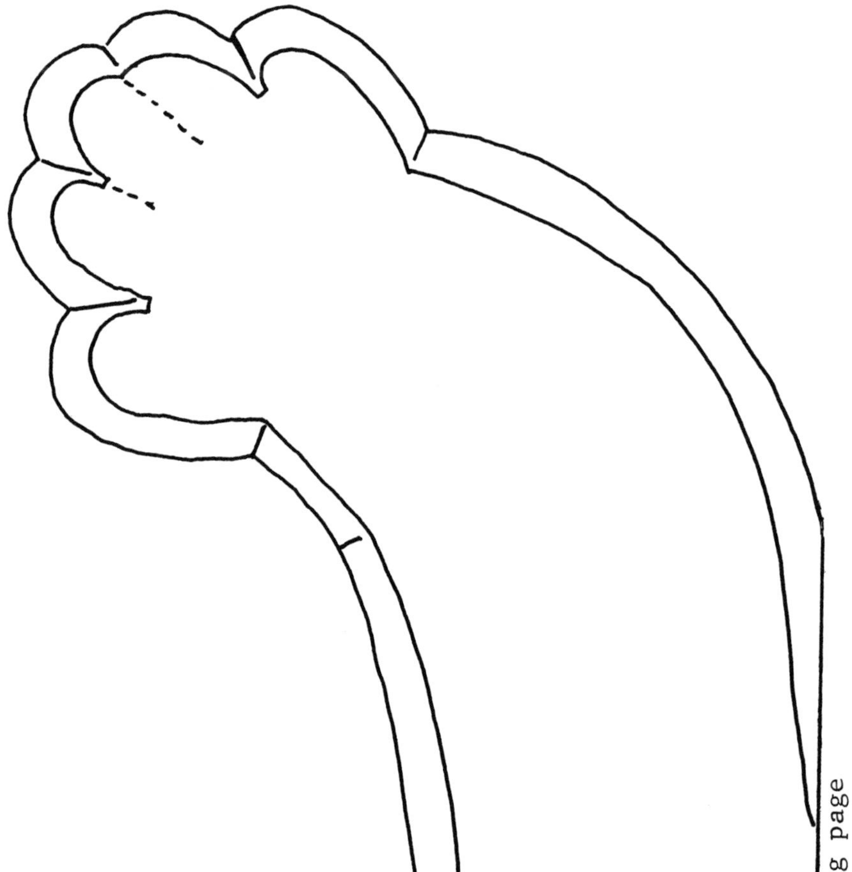

baste along dotted line

fold

join this edge to pattern on the following page

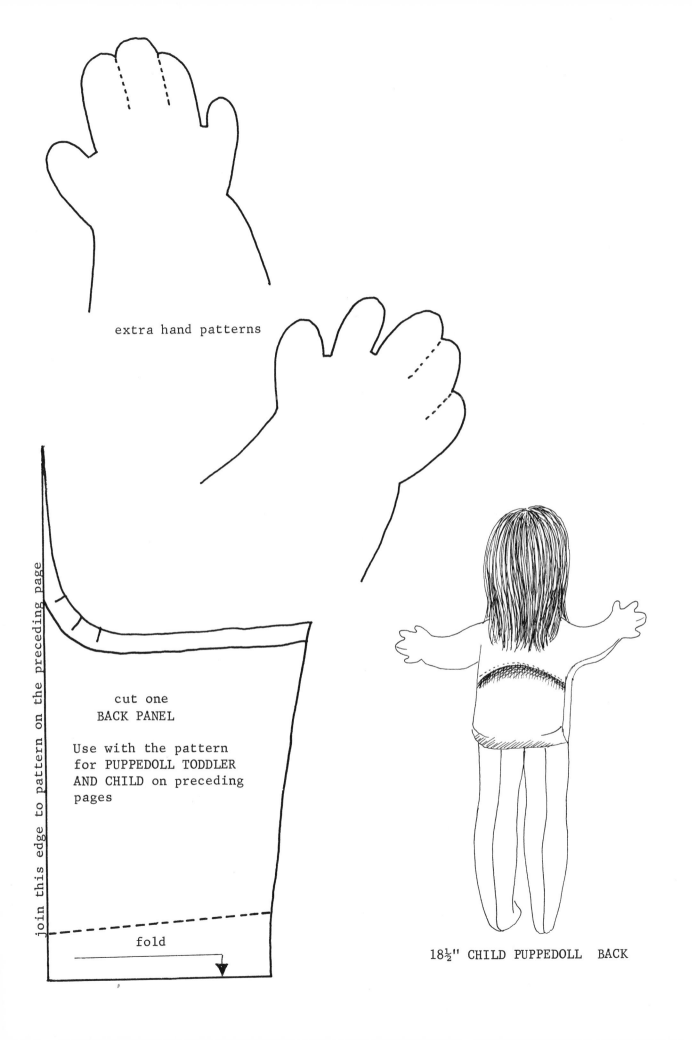

extra hand patterns

join this edge to pattern on the preceding page

cut one
BACK PANEL

Use with the pattern
for PUPPEDOLL TODDLER
AND CHILD on preceding
pages

fold

18½" CHILD PUPPEDOLL BACK

CONSTRUCTING THE PUPPEDOLL™

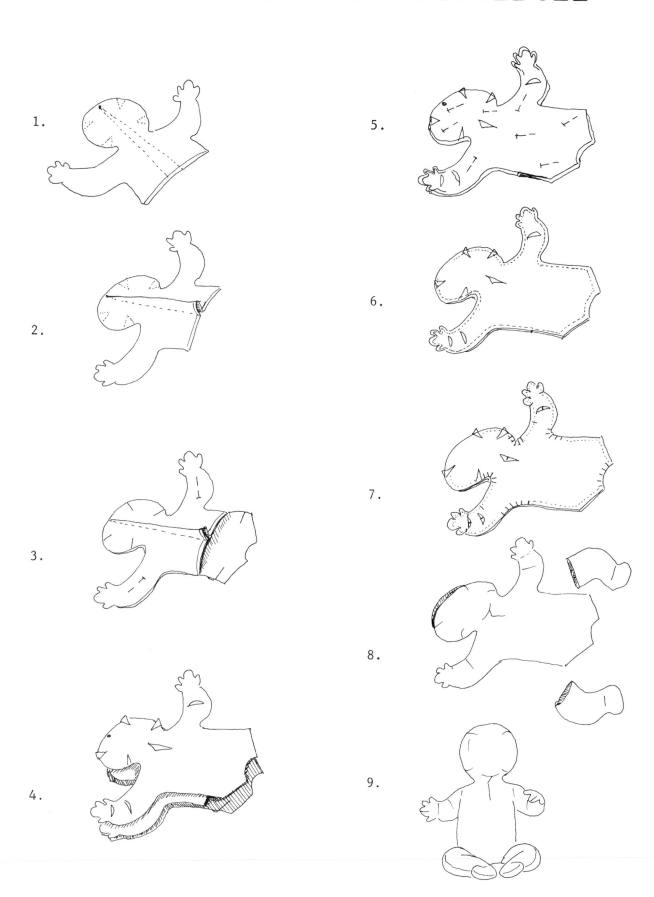

1.

2.

3.

4.

5.

6.

7.

8.

9.

Step 1 shows the back panel for a Baby Puppedoll with the dotted lines marked as indicated on the panel pattern. Hem the bottom edge as shown.

Baste the extra width of the back panel on the dotted lines, with a large stitch, so that the panel is the same size as the front and back pieces as shown in step 2. (The basting will be removed later to make room for your hand.)

Baste or securely pin the back panel to the back piece and treat them as one. Sew the head darts, sewing both panel and back at the same time as shown in step 3. Remember that the panel is on the *outside* so the darts are sewn from the opposite side.

Sew the head, cheek, chin, and arm darts on the *front* piece as shown in step 4. Place the front piece onto the back as shown. The drawing, step 4, shows the front body piece in the air a little above the back piece, rather than lying directly on it, to demonstrate the proper positions of the parts. The back panel and the doll's face should be facing each other with all darts to the outside as shown.

Before sewing the pieces together the hand and finger outlines should be drawn around a cardboard template as suggested for constructing the dolls. Step 5 shows the front and back pieces pinned together with the hand and finger outlines drawn on the front piece.

When sewing the back and front together, start sewing from the head dart and go down the side to the center crotch, then repeat down the other side as shown in step 6, leaving the top of the head open. Sew directly on the hand and finger outlines with your sewing machine's smallest stitch. When you come down in between the separated fingers, *turn and go two stitches across* before turning again and sewing up the side of the next finger.

Step 7 shows the body sewn together with the seams clipped. Clip all the curves between the fingers, the wrists, the crotch, underarms, elbows, and neck as shown. Remember to clip at least once at the widest point of the arm and chin darts as shown.

Turn right-side-out with a small dowel, pushing the fingers out. Remember, when turning the puppedoll, that the back panel is a part of the back piece. The turned Baby Doll with the sewn and turned legs is shown in step 8. Remove the basting from the center of the back panel.

Stuff the puppedoll starting with the fingers, hands and lower arms which should be packed tightly. Stop the packing about one inch from the shoulder line as indicated on the pattern and place a large safety pin at the shoulder to hold the arm stuffing in place.

Pack the hip and tummy space quite firmly using less stuffing as you fill the chest and shoulder areas. *The puppedoll's chest area and neck must be stuffed enough to fill out the form but lightly enough so that it can be squeezed easily and will spring back.* The head must be tightly packed as on the dolls. When the stuffing is done, remove the safety pins from the shoulders. The completed body with the stuffed legs sewn onto it is shown in step 9. Back views of puppedolls, showing the back panel, are illustrated on page 94 and in Plates 41 through 43.

The panel should fit snugly so that getting one's hand into place is like putting on a glove. Hold the panel edge with your other hand and work your fingers up into the arms and head.

I always pin the opening together at the head and put my hand into the puppet panel to see if it is right for me before sewing the opening.

Sometimes I make two rows of top stitching, by hand, at the upper arm and shoulder line, sometimes I don't, as the stuffing usually remains separated where the safety pin has been. When the stitching is used, *you must sew only the front and back pieces together, not the puppedoll panel.* To do this I insert a piece of cardboard, a ruler, or something similar, into the back panel to prevent my needle from catching the panel which must remain open for your hand.

7. Manipulating the Puppedoll™

My basic manipulation instructions are merely to point out the potential for individual expression. Just remember that your puppedoll as puppet will give in direct proportion to what he receives from you. That sounds like a fair exchange doesn't it? Remember, too, that when you tire of that give-and-take relationship all you need do is relax and just enjoy your puppedoll as a doll.

The standard 15-inch Baby, the 17-inch Toddler, and the 18½-inch Child Puppedolls are designed primarily for older children and adult hands. Although a small child can manipulate the head and one arm with ease, the adult-size hand can realize the puppedoll's maximum potential.

The Little Baby and Little Toddler Puppedolls are designed primarily for small hands. Even very young children have enough finger span to manipulate both arms and head at the same time. Adults simply leave one or two fingers outside during manipulation. In other words, both small children and adults can work both sizes of puppedolls. The standard hand and finger position is shown on page 94.

Some puppeteers prefer another hand position for working a puppedoll with the index finger and the two middle fingers, (the second and third) all in the back of the head with the thumb in one arm and the little finger into the other. Still others have told me they like the index finger and the next, the second finger in the head with the thumb in one arm and the third and fourth fingers in the other arm.

I have seen some of my friends, men with very large hands, work the 15-inch Baby puppedoll in the manner a woman works the Little Baby puppedoll. You will find what is most comfortable and natural for you in order to realize the maximum creative potential.

My two college-age daughters, Anne and Elizabeth, who have performed with the Opryland, U.S.A. puppeteers for five summers, had their own puppet troop for four years before that, during high school. They are totally at ease with puppets and sometimes, when in the mood to experiment and create, will pick up one of my puppedolls and literally make it "come alive"!

The puppedoll not only can sit on your hand, as in Plates 45 through 49, while you work him with your other hand, but he can also sit on your lap as illustrated on page 95. You can manipulate him as you cradle him in your arms or even hold him upright at your shoulder as shown also. You can sit him on someone else's shoulder and let him "talk" to someone and, of course, you can always sit him on the arm or back of a chair or sofa.

I mustn't forget to mention that in addition to all this, the puppedoll can still be manipulated in all the traditional puppet ways—on stage, over a folding screen, from behind a chair—and he is very good on movie and television film, too!

The puppedoll can, for instance, rub its eyes, brush its hair back, suck its thumb, clap its hands, play with its feet, cover its face, move its head "yes" or "no," twist its head, look side to side, shrug its shoulders, lay its head down, throw its head back, cover its eyes and ears, raise its hands over its head, rub its tummy, scratch its head, reach out to touch someone, throw kisses (whew!) and these are only *some* of the basic movements he is capable of, with your help. When one combines these movements and increases in skill with only a little practice, there is no end to the lifelike things the puppedolls can do.

Pattern page 96 shows several accessories you can use for your puppedoll such as a bassinet, a papoose, infant seat or a fancy pillow. All you need do is make an opening in the back for your hand.

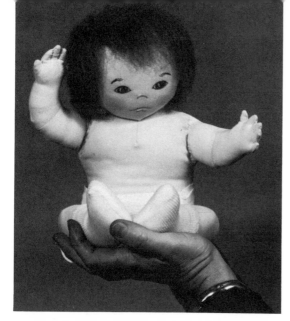

Plate 45. The Puppedoll Baby can spread his arms . . .

Plate 46. . . . clap his hands . . .

Plate 47. . . . play with his foot . . .

Plate 48. . . . suck his thumb . . .

Plate 49. . . . and twist his head, or shrug his shoulders, to illustrate just a few of the many lifelike things he is capable of doing with your help.

MANIPULATING THE PUPPEDOLL™

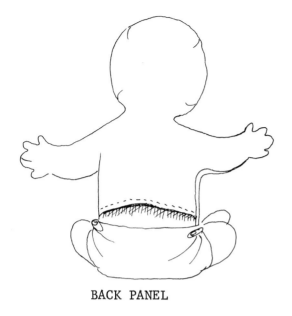

BACK PANEL

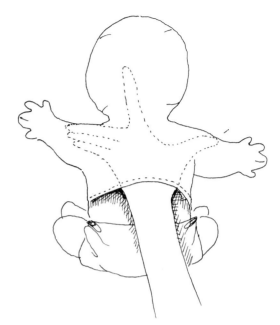

POSITION OF HUMAN HAND

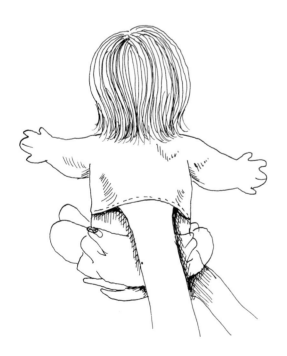

COMPLETED PUPPEDOLL BABY

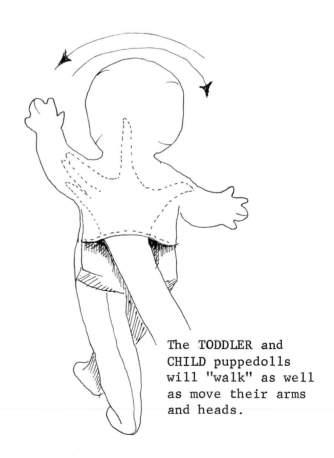

The TODDLER and CHILD puppedolls will "walk" as well as move their arms and heads.

Manipulate your puppedoll as you cradle it in your arms, or as he sits on some other surface such as a chair arm or back.

The shoulder position offers many possibilities for creativity as does the lap position.

Manipulate your puppedoll
through an opening in a basket,
a papoose, infant seat or
pillow for use in theatre
productions as well as
for play.

8. The Teddy Bear Family

Not only did the Teddy bear originate in America, but it was named for an American president—Teddy Roosevelt. That was during the early part of the twentieth century and it is still one of the most beloved toys of all time in America, England, parts of Europe, and possibly even Russia! There's a "rumor" that as many bears are sold for adults as for children! Some people have even stated that there are *more* of the lovable creatures sold for adults than for children. We do know, for a fact, that most Teddy bears are sold *to* adults, and who knows how many of them are *for* the grown-ups as well?

The bears invite you to love them and when you do they respond with warmth, softness, and a lovable expression. If anything in this world cries out for, even *commands* that we touch it, it's the Teddy bear!

PABEAR

Pabear, Plate 6, is 18 inches tall. His bear nose is a circle of the same fur cloth as his body, gathered slightly and stuffed with polyester or cotton stuffing. It is sewn securely to his face, by hand, all the way around.

The front part of his ears, his nose, the inside of his paws, and the bottom of his feet are the same ⅝-inch pile fur fabric as the rest of him, but the pile has been clipped almost all the way down to the cloth backing. The clipped cloth becomes darker than the fur but it coordinates perfectly, of course. The clipping is like any other haircut or clipping in that it gives each bear you create his own unique look. I always do the "grooming" after the bear is assembled. It only takes a few moments. The hand-crafted, individual grooming gives a bear a certain "class" which can't easily be bought in a store and it's great fun to do. It provides excitement in the same way that making the wig and embroidering a doll's face do. You can groom your bear still more by brushing him with a hairbrush.

Pabear wears a crochet muffler and a stocking cap.

The pattern for Pabear is given on pages 99 through 102.

MABEAR

The mama bear, whom I call Mabear is 15½ inches tall and made of the same light brown ⅝-inch pile fur. She has her fur clipped and groomed on her ears, nose and paws just as Pabear has.

Her nose is made of two separate pieces but can be interchanged with Pabear's round one if you prefer. Her nose can be used plain or with a little pink mouth sewn into the seam. She has "real" eyelashes glued above her button eyes.

Most of the clothes for the Baby, Toddler, and Child dolls will fit Mabear if made just a bit fatter in the arms and legs. Her dress, shown in Plate 6, is made from the baby christening dress pattern. I used a patchwork patterned cotton for a country look and added a simple muslin apron. The mob cap in Plate 3 is charming on her if you want her to have a hat.

Plate 50 shows this same 15½-inch middle-sized bear dressed as a boy bear which can be used as a smaller size papa, too. He wears a red bandana and blue denim overalls made from the doll overalls pattern. Slide the pattern about 1 inch back from the fold edge when you cut, to add width to the legs. I make the straps a little fatter, too.

The pattern for Mabear is given on pages 103 through 106.

BABEAR

The 11½-inch baby bear has curved legs to give him a cuddly baby look. (Plate 6) Babear is made of a soft, short-pile, fur cloth, (about ¼-inch pile). His nose is like that of Pabear.

He can wear the clothes for Little Baby doll if the sleeves and legs are made a bit fatter for him. In Plate 6 he wears a crochet cap to match his little crochet muffler.

The curves of his body and the softness of his fur make this bear an absolute delight to hold in your hands!

The pattern for Babear is given on pages 107 and 108.

BITTY BEAR

My smallest bear, 8-inch Bitty Bear, is shown in two very different interpretations in Plate 50. On the left he is made of a soft, silky, brown fur longer than that used for the Bitty Bear on the right. The brown fur pile is about ½ inch deep while the tan fur pile of the other Bitty is only about ¼ inch deep. The Bitty Bear in the overalls is made from the same fur cloth as the 11½-inch Babear in Plate 6.

Although I do give the fur pile depth in the descriptions, remember that although it is important it is just as important, or even more so, to consider the thickness and stiffness of the fur backing. One simple rule to remember is "the smaller the bear, the softer the fur." In making the smaller size bears you can use a long pile if the *density* of the pile is light.

Bitty Bear wears the clothes for the Little Bitty Baby doll on page 39, made a little fatter for him to compensate for the thickness of the fur.

This smallest size bear can be a baby for any of the larger size bears. He makes a great Teddy bear for any of the dolls in my American Children series in Plates 1 through 4, and 9.

The pattern for Bitty Bear is given on page 109.

Plate 50. Billy Bear is a middle-sized bear and is dressed in denim overalls and a red bandanna. With him are two Bitty Bears, Boo, on the left and Buzz on the right.

PABEAR

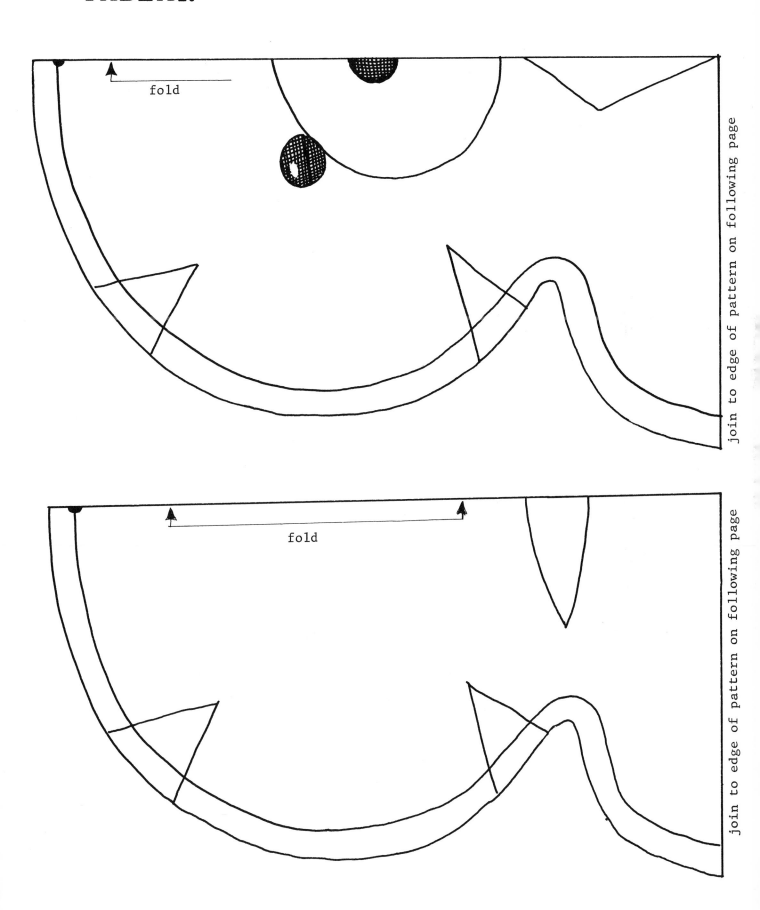

fold

fold

join to edge of pattern on following page

join to edge of pattern on following page

PABEAR

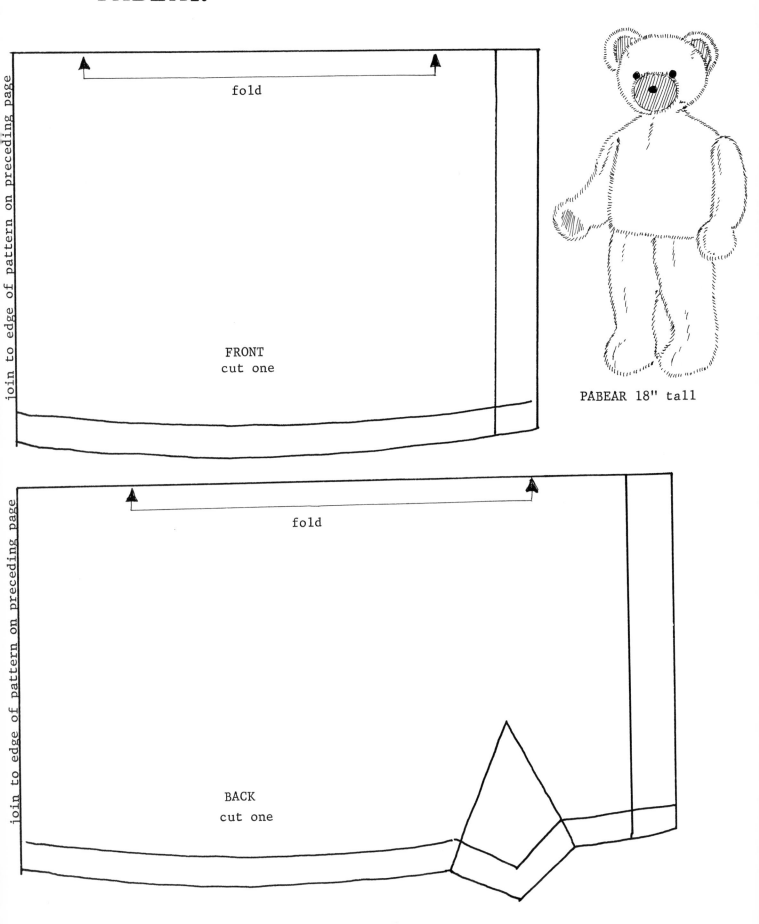

fold

FRONT
cut one

PABEAR 18" tall

fold

BACK
cut one

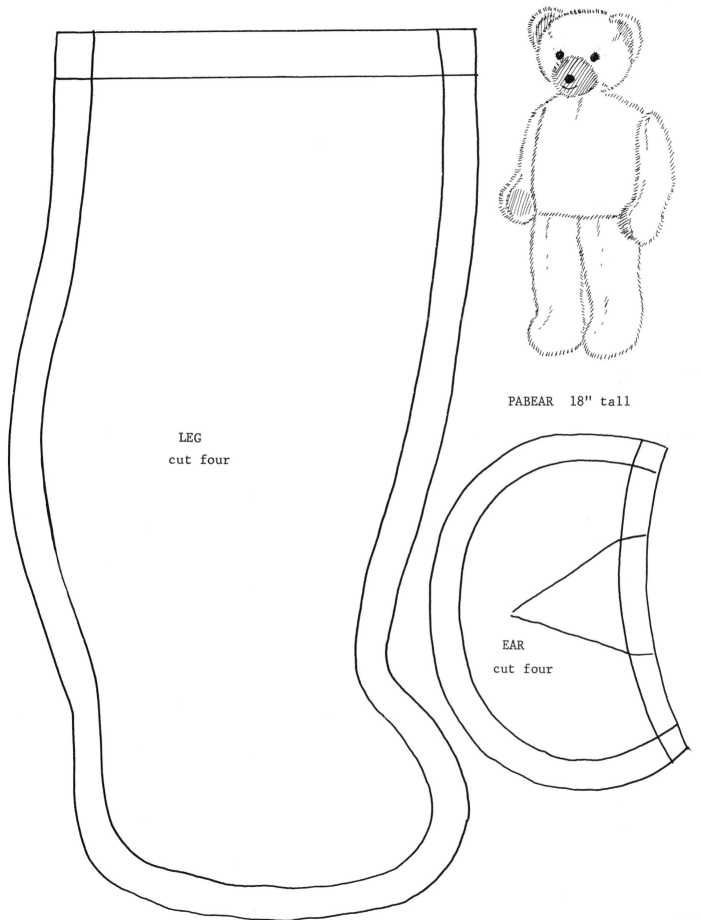

LEG
cut four

PABEAR 18" tall

EAR
cut four

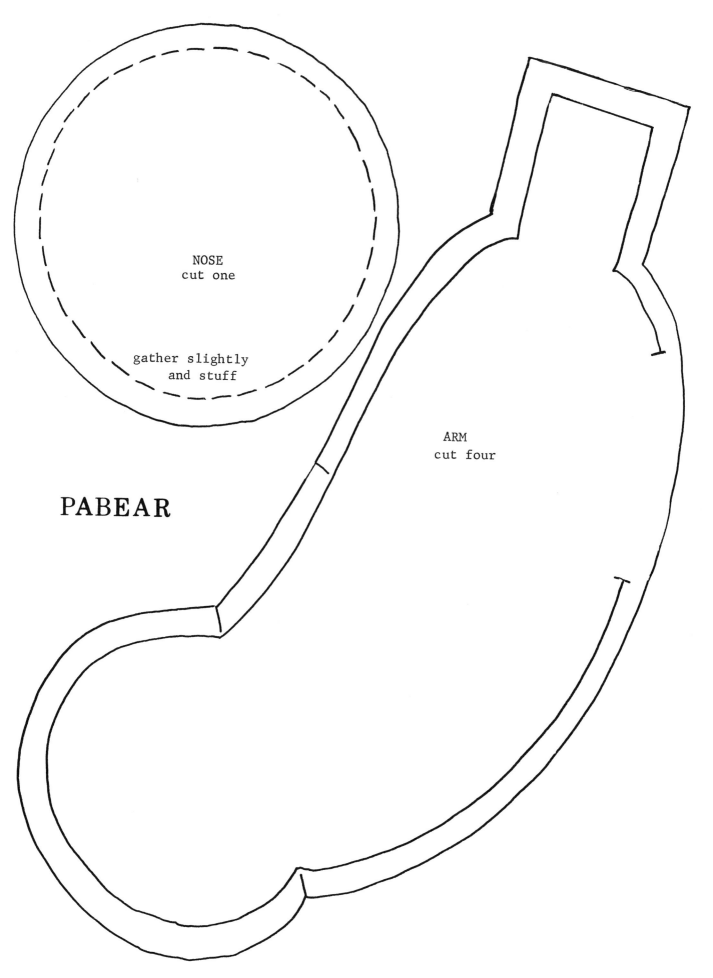

NOSE
cut one

gather slightly
and stuff

ARM
cut four

PABEAR

MABEAR

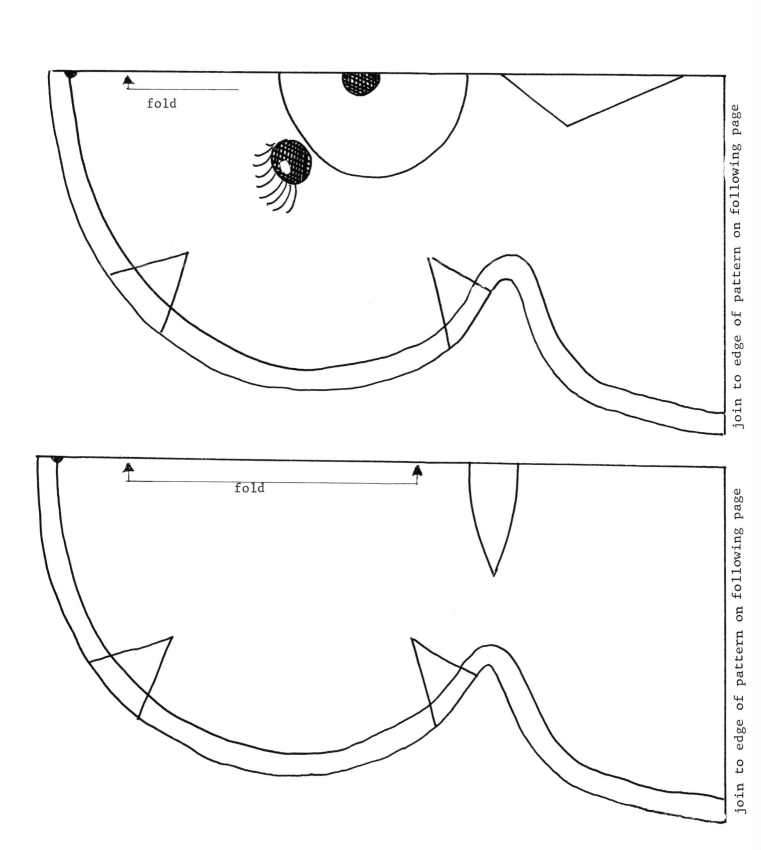

fold

fold

join to edge of pattern on following page

join to edge of pattern on following page

103

MABEAR

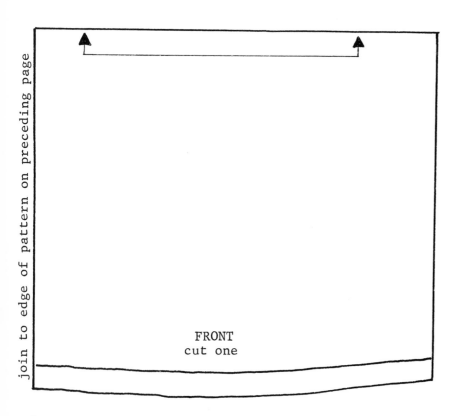

FRONT
cut one

join to edge of pattern on preceding page

MABEAR 15½" tall

She can wear dresses made
from the BABY, TODDLER and
CHILD DOLL clothes patterns.
The sleeves may need to be
made a little looser to
compensate for the thickness
of the fur cloth.

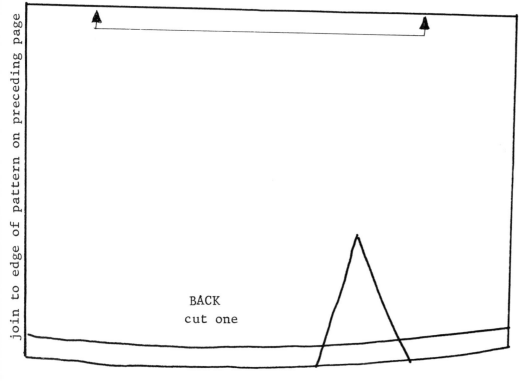

BACK
cut one

join to edge of pattern on preceding page

A MEDIUM-SIZE BOY BEAR
15½" tall

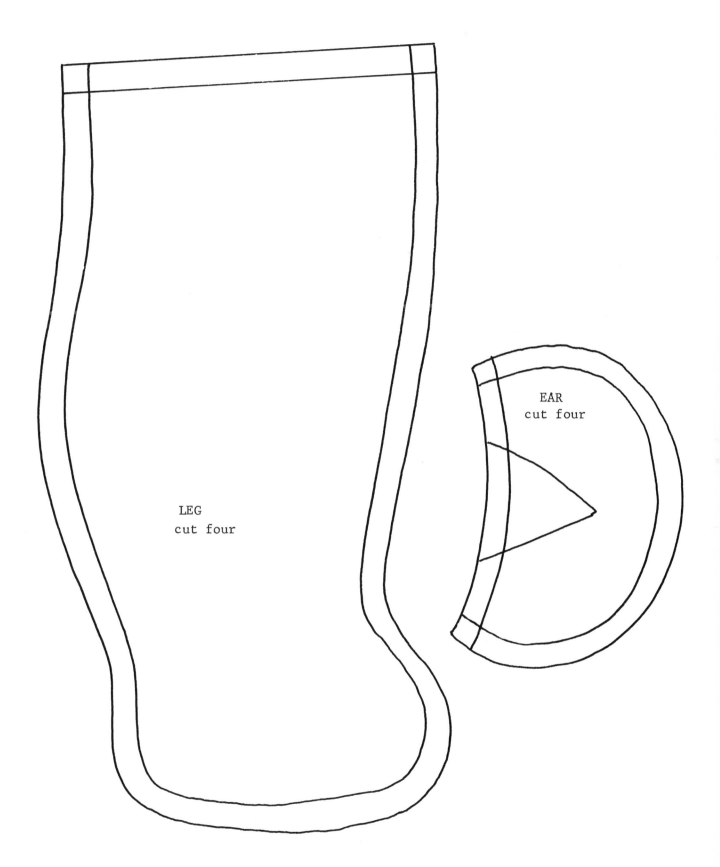

LEG
cut four

EAR
cut four

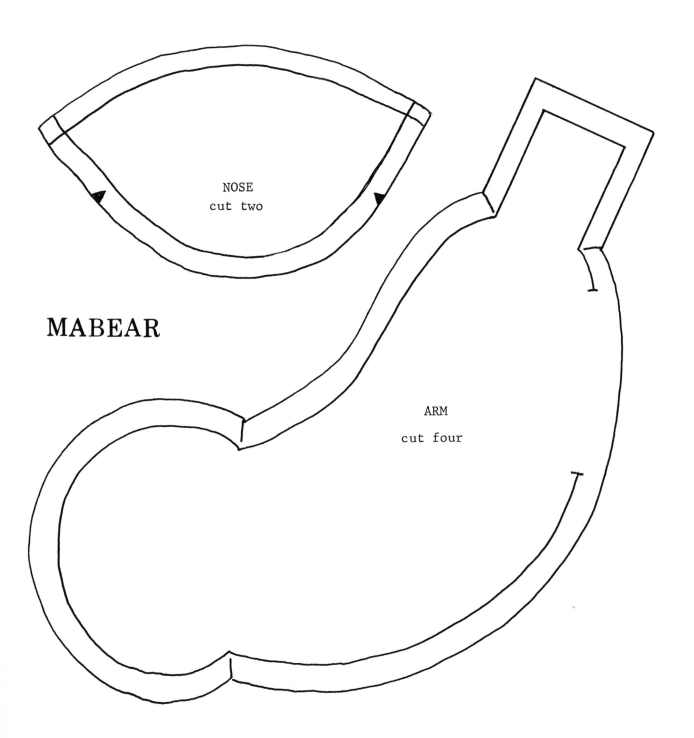

NOSE
cut two

MABEAR

ARM

cut four

BABEAR

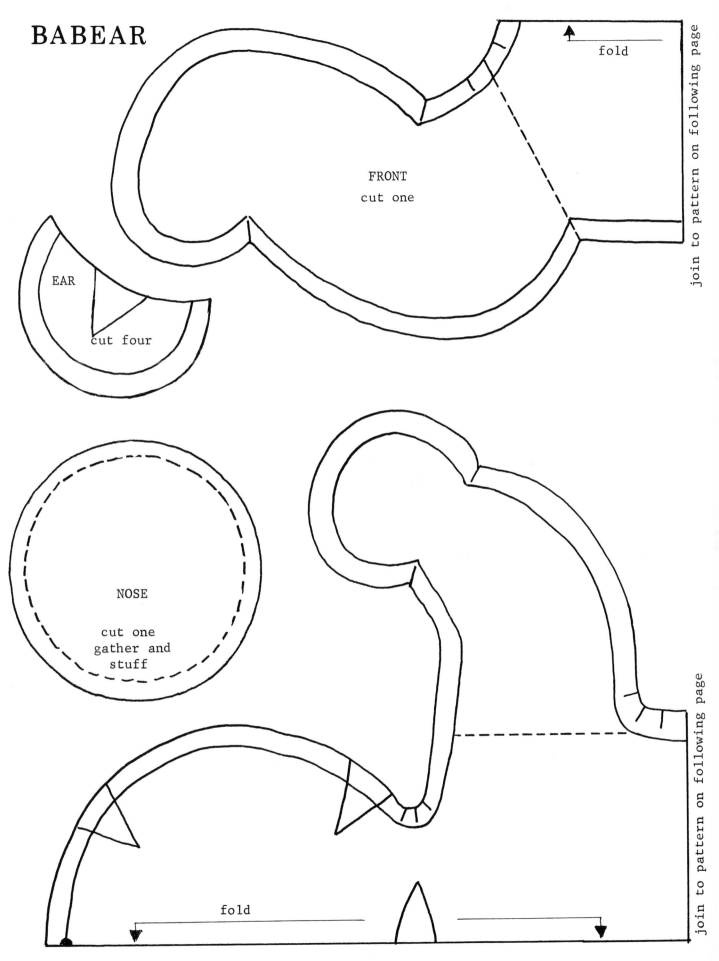

FRONT
cut one

EAR

cut four

NOSE

cut one
gather and
stuff

fold

fold

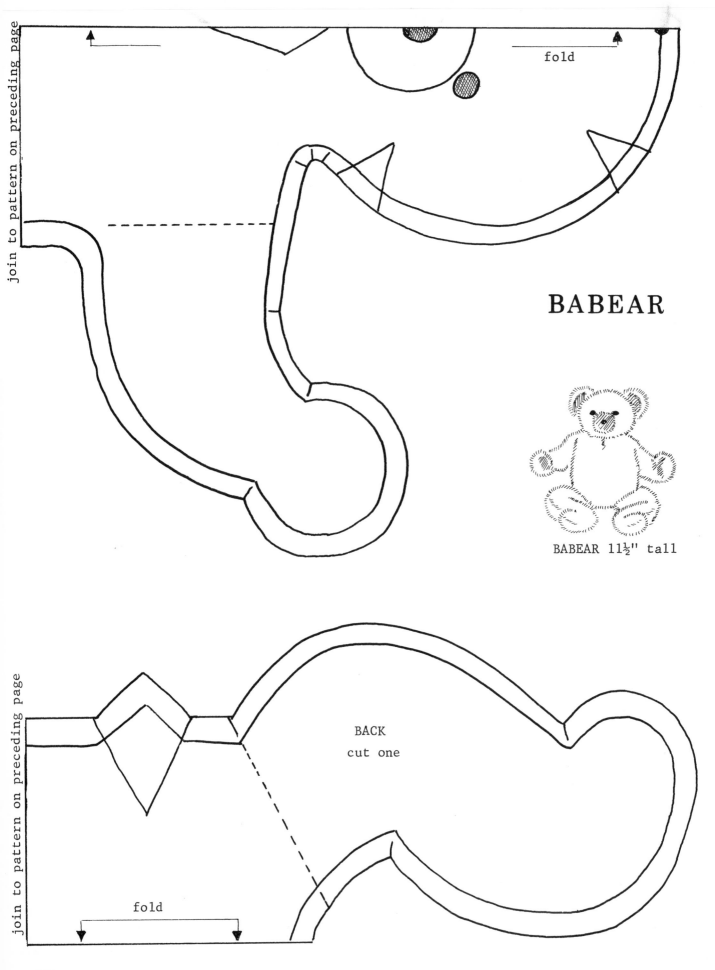

fold

join to pattern on preceding page

BABEAR

BABEAR 11½" tall

BACK
cut one

fold

join to pattern on preceding page

108

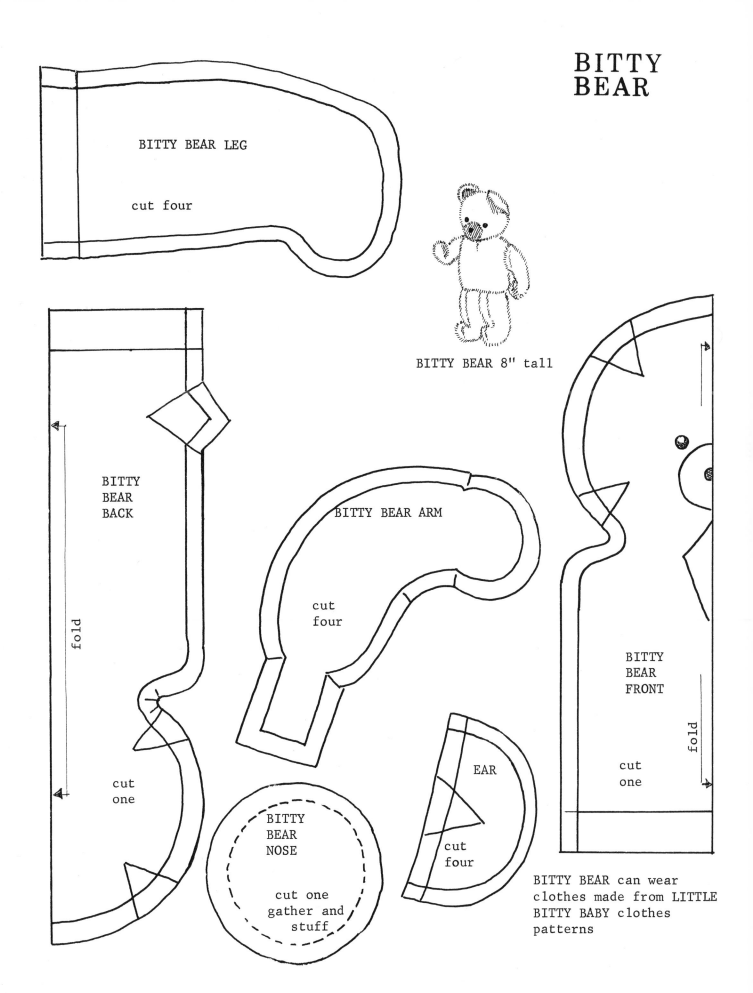

BITTY
BEAR

BITTY BEAR LEG

cut four

BITTY BEAR 8" tall

BITTY
BEAR
BACK

fold

cut
one

BITTY BEAR ARM

cut
four

BITTY
BEAR
NOSE

cut one
gather and
stuff

EAR

cut
four

BITTY
BEAR
FRONT

fold

cut
one

BITTY BEAR can wear
clothes made from LITTLE
BITTY BABY clothes
patterns

9. Fashion Dolls

The slender fashion dolls of today are nothing new. Fashion dolls have been around for centuries! Until ladies' fashion magazines came along after the Civil War, the fashion doll had been one way to display the latest clothing designs. They were for adults originally but young girls owned them, too.

My fashion dolls include a woman about 17 inches tall, a girl about 14 inches, and a child about 11 inches with basic patterns for designing your own clothes. Patterns for the dolls and their clothes are given on pages 112 to 122.

The woman doll has round hips and shapely legs, shown in Plate 51, so that she can wear modern clothes such as the pants suit in Plate 52.

All three fashion dolls can wear the period clothes shown in my book, *The Doll Book*, if they are enlarged 1½ times. Draw a grid over the *Doll Book* patterns with the squares each ½ inch square. Enlarge the clothes onto another grid with each square ¾ inch. The book has American clothes from 1660 to 1910 and hair styles in every period, too. The only alterations needed will be in the long sleeves. These fashion dolls have longer arms of more real-life proportions than my smaller dolls.

The woman in Plate 7 wears an 1890s Gibson Girl skirt and blouse. The girl and child dolls wear basic dresses which can be adapted to many periods by shortening or lengthening the bodices. The patterns include pants which can be adapted for pantaloons, flared pants, fitted pants, jeans, pajamas, or jumpsuits for any period you might want.

PORTRAIT AND CHARACTER DOLLS

These dolls are easily adapted to represent persons of today or of the past. The modern doll of Plates 35 and 52, whom I call Rosalynn because of her dark hair and slim figure, could be a Rosalynn Carter, First Lady Doll. The blonde child of Plate 7, with her hair worn longer could be an Amy Carter doll. I have done several Minnie Pearl and Dolly Parton country music star dolls as well as historical women such as Martha Washington and Dolly Madison.

If you are interested in doing famous people dolls, it is a good idea to start a file of newspaper and magazine clippings and pictures of anyone whom you think you might want to portray. The file can prove invaluable when you set out to work on the doll! I have clippings of several inaugurations of presidents and Tennessee governors in my file, a number of them in color. With character dolls, it's easier to think ahead than to have to do a lot of research when you find the time to do that doll you've been planning.

The two children fashion dolls are suitable for portrait children because, although of a miniature scale, they are large enough to allow you to really create a likeness. These bodies can be used for boy children as well as girls. You can modify the length of the arms, legs, or bodies to further create an impression of someone in particular.

There really is so much that can be done with the Fashion Dolls that it could fill another whole book! I hope that you will use them as the basis for some of those dolls you've been planning to make but haven't gotten around to.

If you have never designed your own doll's fashions before, you might find my book *Early American Costume*, (Stackpole, 1975) of value. It not only has two hundred seventy years of American clothing, but a chapter on how to draft your own patterns as well.

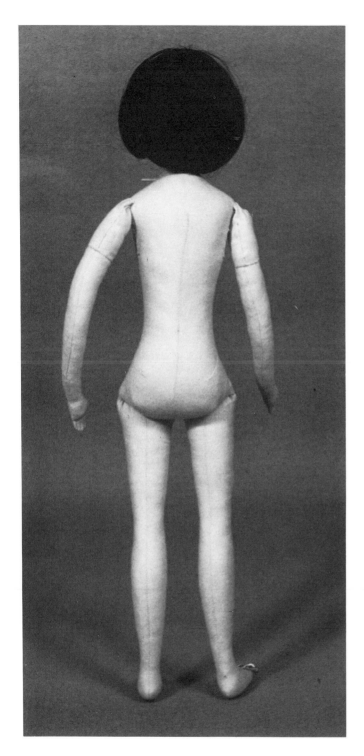

Plate 51. The Fashion Doll woman seen from the rear to show her modern figure.

Plate 52. Rosalynn shows how the Fashion Doll woman can be used as a portrait or character doll.

FASHION DOLL WOMAN

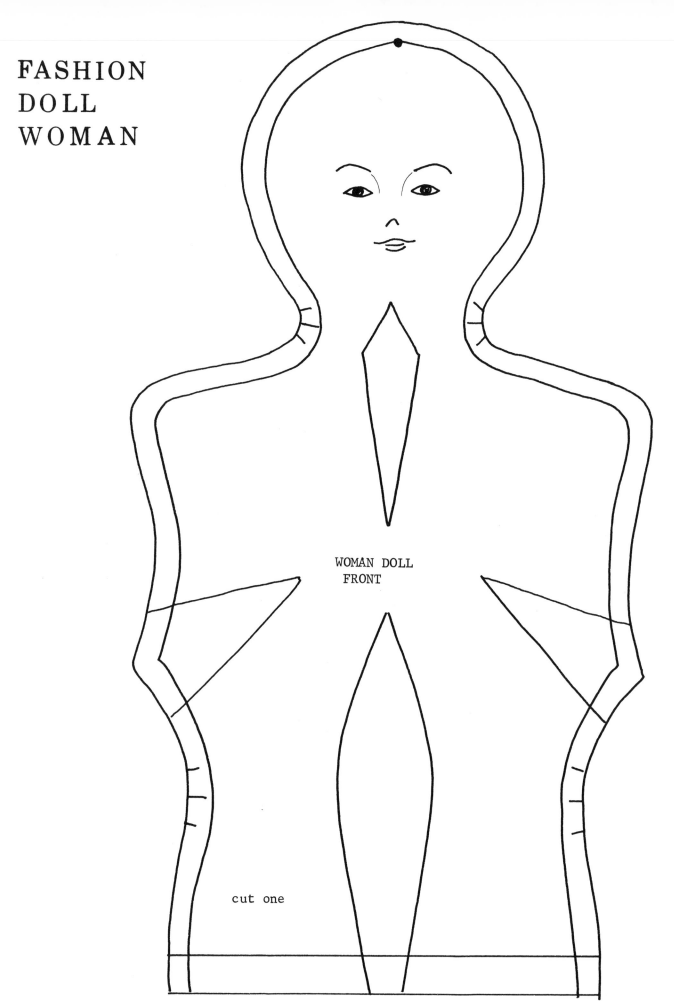

WOMAN DOLL
FRONT

cut one

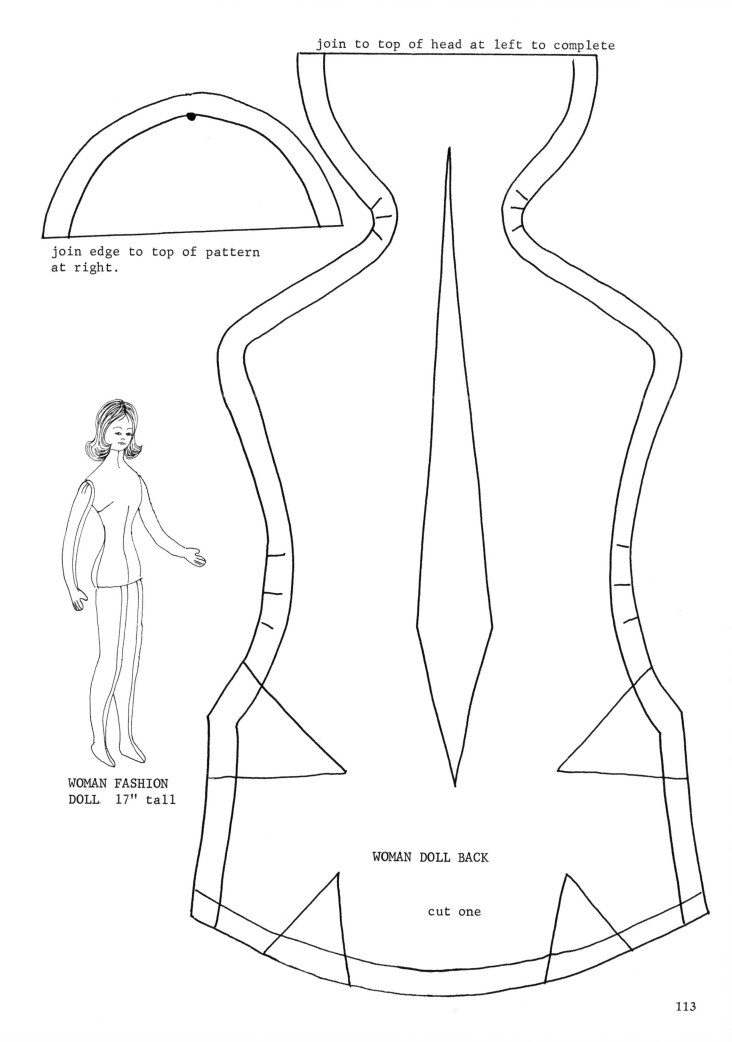

join to top of head at left to complete

join edge to top of pattern at right.

WOMAN FASHION DOLL 17" tall

WOMAN DOLL BACK

cut one

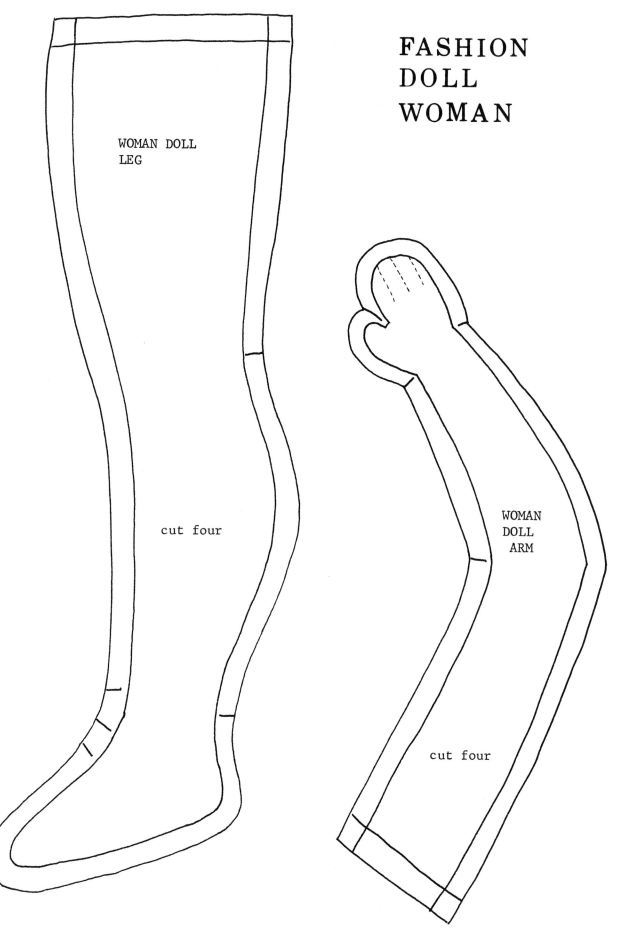

FASHION
DOLL
WOMAN

WOMAN DOLL
LEG

cut four

WOMAN
DOLL
ARM

cut four

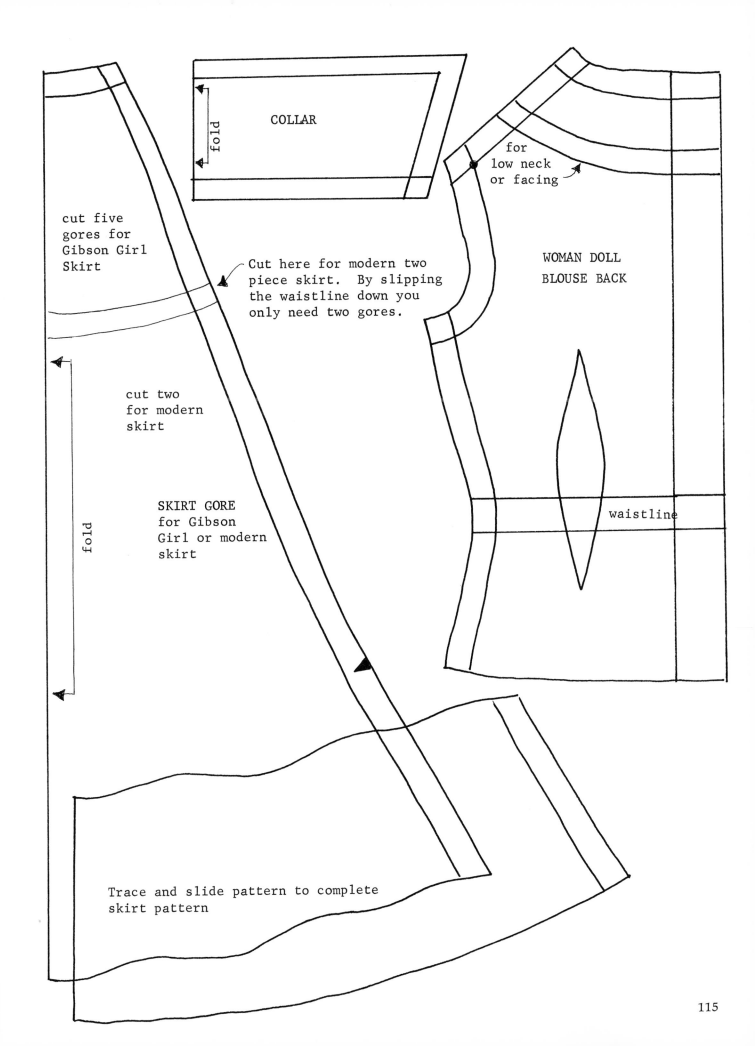

COLLAR

fold

for
low neck
or facing

WOMAN DOLL
BLOUSE BACK

cut five
gores for
Gibson Girl
Skirt

Cut here for modern two
piece skirt. By slipping
the waistline down you
only need two gores.

cut two
for modern
skirt

fold

SKIRT GORE
for Gibson
Girl or modern
skirt

waistline

Trace and slide pattern to complete
skirt pattern

115

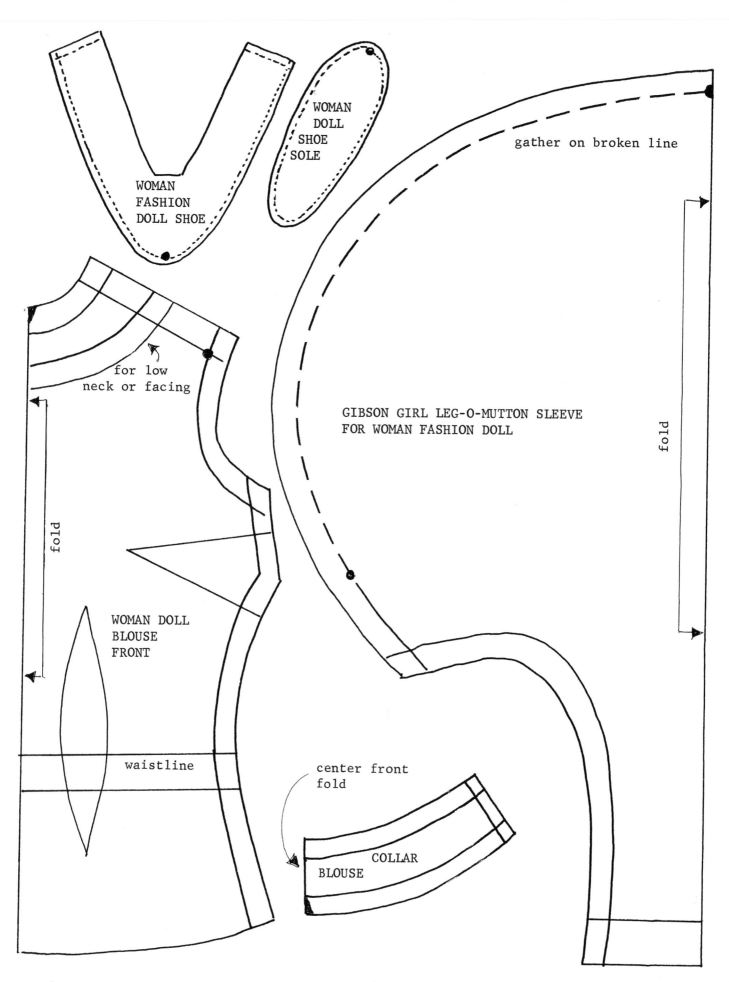

WOMAN
DOLL
SHOE
SOLE

WOMAN
FASHION
DOLL SHOE

gather on broken line

for low
neck or facing

fold

GIBSON GIRL LEG-O-MUTTON SLEEVE
FOR WOMAN FASHION DOLL

fold

fold

WOMAN DOLL
BLOUSE
FRONT

waistline

center front
fold

COLLAR

BLOUSE

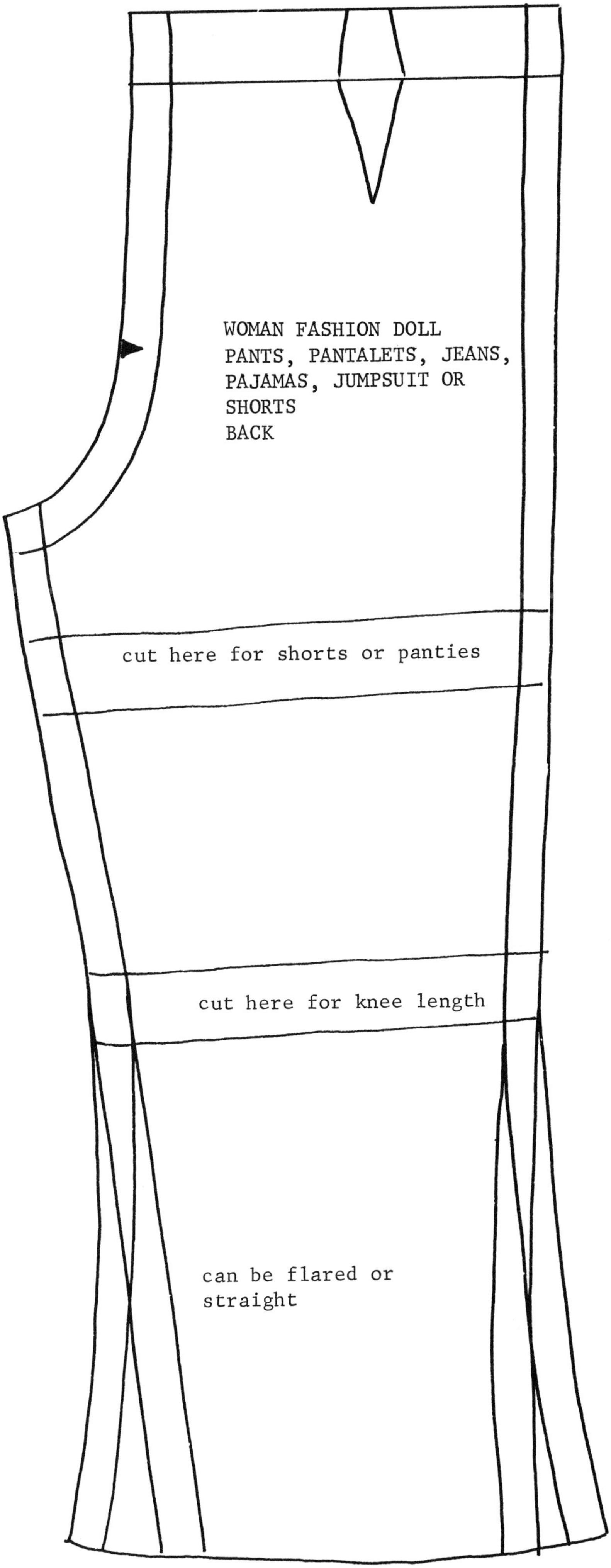

WOMAN FASHION DOLL
PANTS, PANTALETS, JEANS,
PAJAMAS, JUMPSUIT OR
SHORTS
BACK

cut here for shorts or panties

cut here for knee length

can be flared or
straight

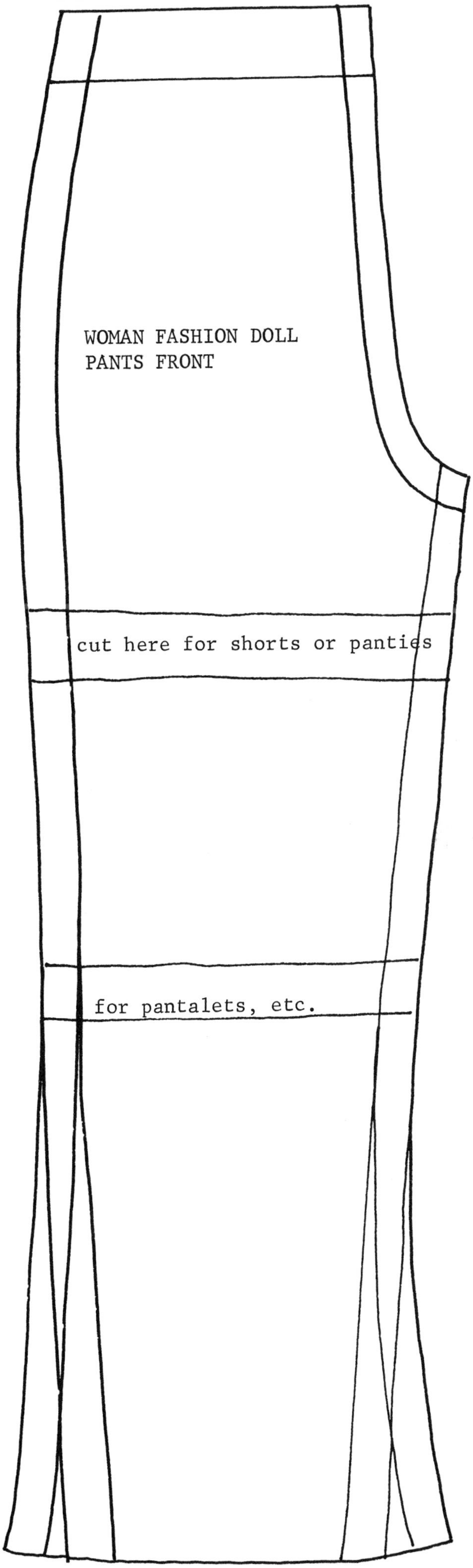

WOMAN FASHION DOLL
PANTS FRONT

cut here for shorts or panties

for pantalets, etc.

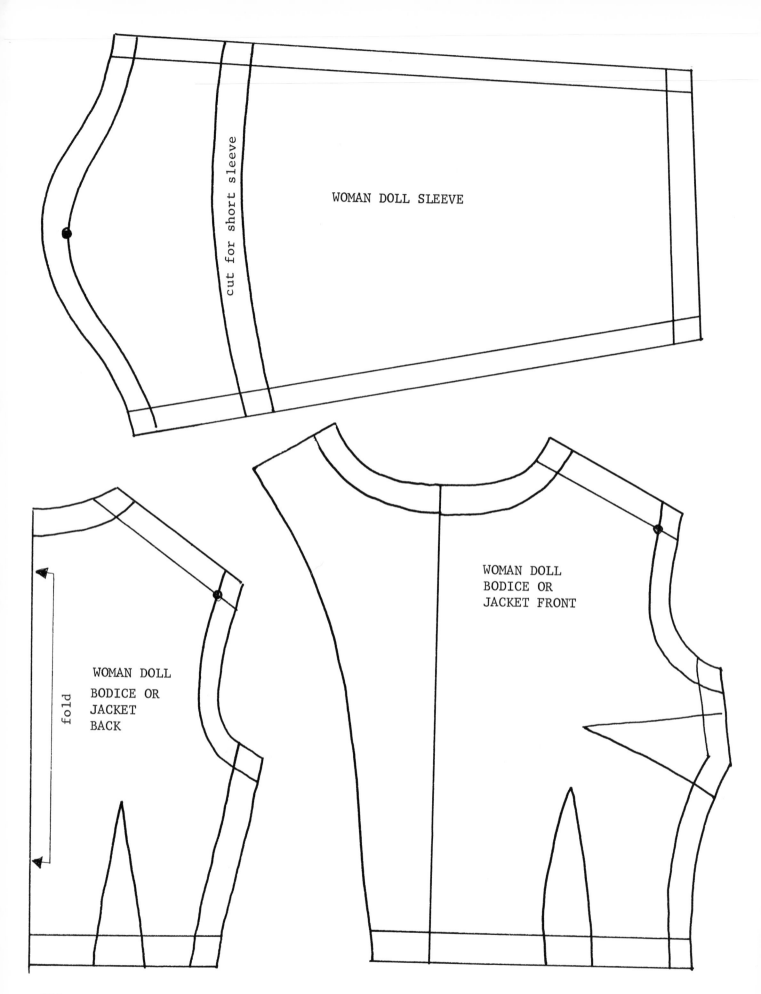

WOMAN DOLL SLEEVE

cut for short sleeve

WOMAN DOLL
BODICE OR
JACKET
BACK

fold

WOMAN DOLL
BODICE OR
JACKET FRONT

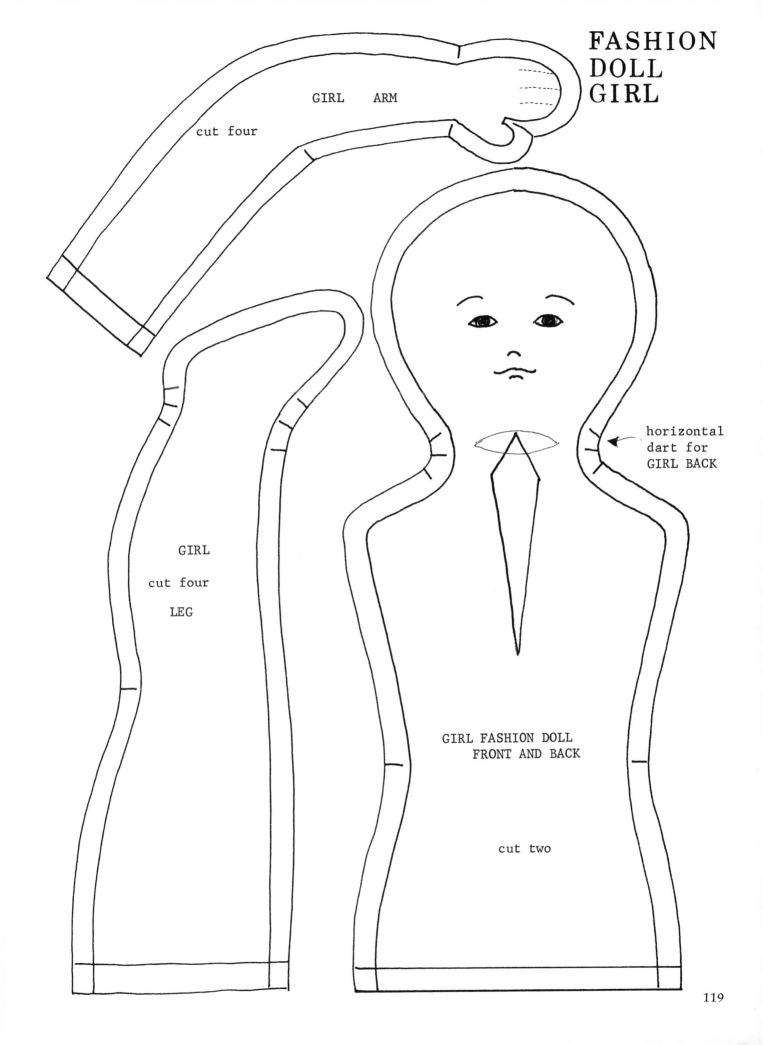

FASHION
DOLL
GIRL

GIRL   ARM

cut four

GIRL

cut four

LEG

horizontal
dart for
GIRL BACK

GIRL FASHION DOLL
FRONT AND BACK

cut two

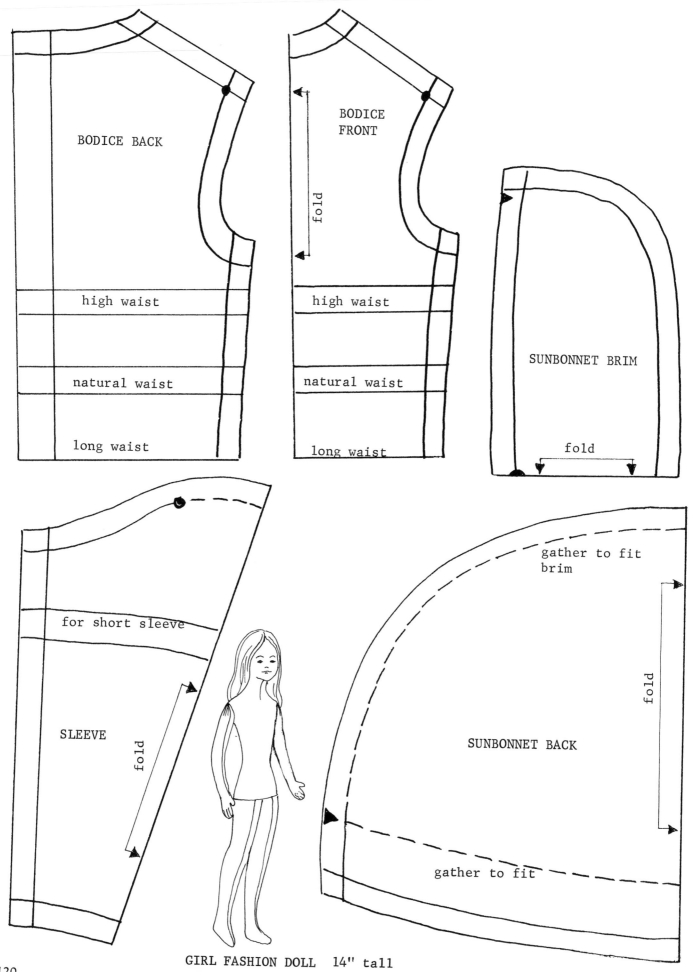

BODICE BACK

BODICE FRONT

fold

high waist

natural waist

long waist

high waist

natural waist

long waist

SUNBONNET BRIM

fold

for short sleeve

SLEEVE

fold

gather to fit brim

fold

SUNBONNET BACK

gather to fit

GIRL FASHION DOLL   14" tall

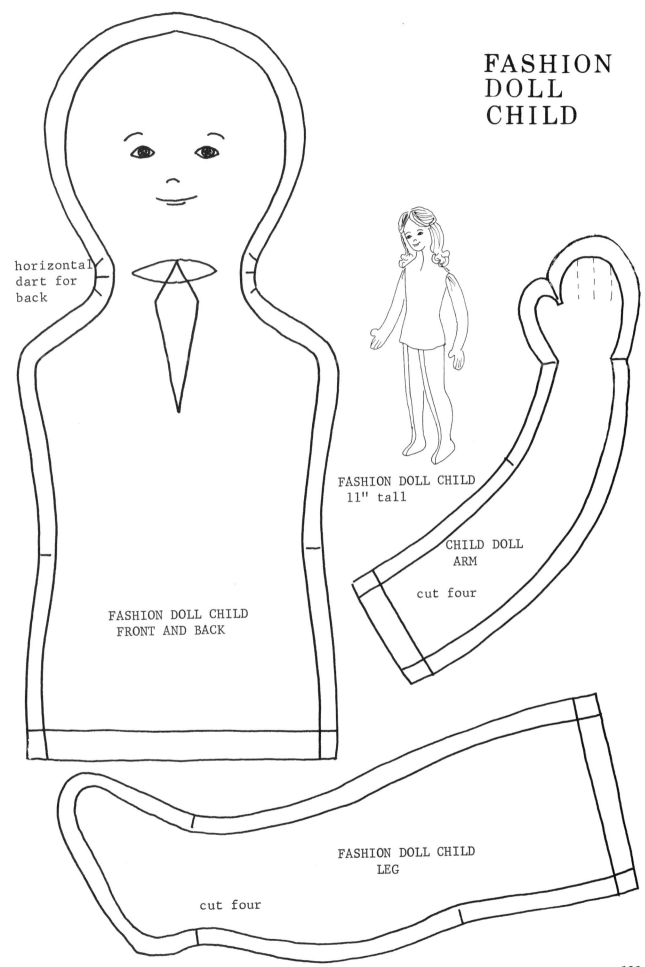

FASHION DOLL CHILD

horizontal dart for back

FASHION DOLL CHILD
FRONT AND BACK

FASHION DOLL CHILD
11" tall

CHILD DOLL
ARM

cut four

FASHION DOLL CHILD
LEG

cut four

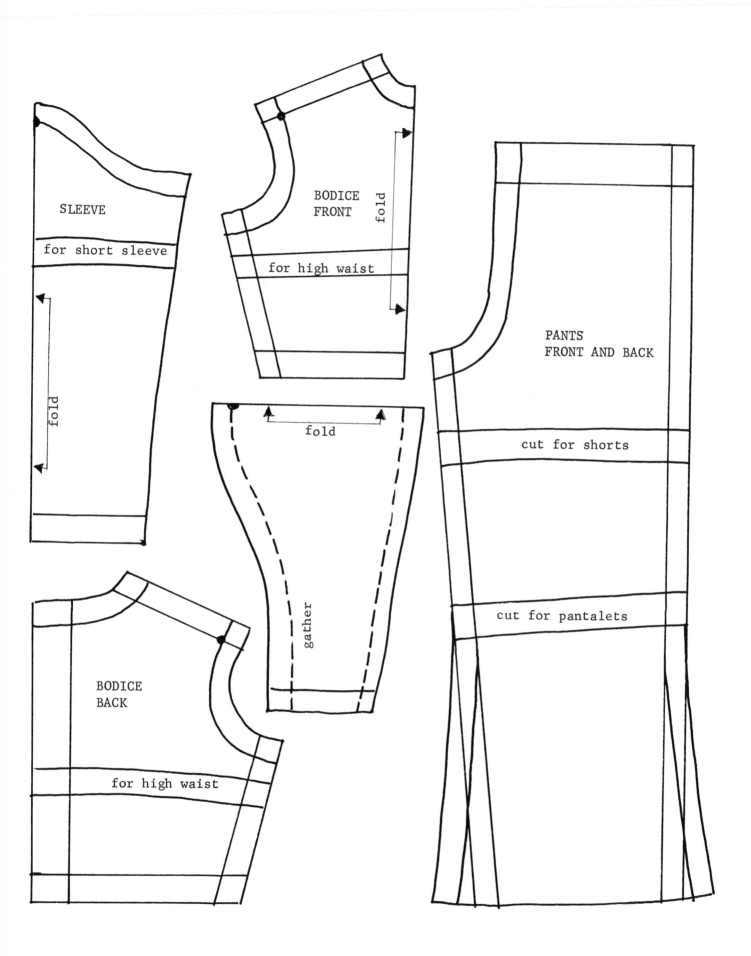

SLEEVE

for short sleeve

fold

BODICE
FRONT

fold

for high waist

fold

gather

BODICE
BACK

for high waist

PANTS
FRONT AND BACK

cut for shorts

cut for pantalets

122

10. Old Timeys

Many antique dolls were actually purchased in parts. Often only the head, hands and feet were bought, sometimes from different companies. The body was then made by a family member or a dressmaker. Because many of these people had little or no knowledge of anatomy they often used rather distorted proportions. Sometimes, I'm sure, they simply wanted a doll to be a certain size and, using what hands and feet they could find, went ahead and deliberately constructed the doll that size even though the parts were a different scale. The range of proportions in dolls is very wide.

I am not criticizing the old dolls; I wouldn't change them for anything. I love them just the way they are—so much, in fact, that I decided to use them as inspiration. My "Old Timeys" are certainly not meant to be imitations of old dolls or of other materials. They are just light-hearted cloth interpretations which capture something of the essence of the old dolls. They are, what I call, a simple "Gingerbread Man" construction involving just two pieces; a front and a back. They do have little darts at the neck and the addition of a bun of hair at the head to give them depth along with their simplicity.

Both the back and front darts are on the same pattern as they are the only difference between the front and back pattern pieces. The vertical dart is for the front as it forms the neck, chin, and chest. The horizontal dart is for the back of the head and neck.

The Old Timeys' character comes from their design, the way the cloth is cut in order to achieve just the right angle of the arms and legs.

The heads and shoulders are painted with at least four coats of white liquid glue to give them the feeling of china, papier-mâché, wax, or wood. Their hair and shoes are painted on to further add to their period look. One of the dolls, Lucy, was painted with a coat of wax over the glue and she has human hair.

Their features are painted with felt-tip pens (the indelible kind), color pencils, or oil colors. (Be sure to test your paints on a piece of cloth to see that they don't run.)

Their noses are the tiniest triangles of pink felt glued onto the face before the several coats of glue were applied.

Glue can be used on the hands and feet as well as the head, making them hard. You can just dip the feet in black paint for the shoes and boots, or use a mixture of glue with ink for coloring. It is fun to experiment with these little dolls as they require such little time and money; just be sure to test all paints and colors on a scrap of cloth before trying them on your doll.

For a china doll interpretation, you might want to use a white cloth instead of pink and for the wooden doll try a tan or cream color. You'll have fun as long as you don't take them too seriously. Just remember that they should be a mimic or a cartoon rather than a serious attempt to be something they are not. Use your cloth to help capture something of the old dolls but don't try to pass it off for another material and above all, have fun!

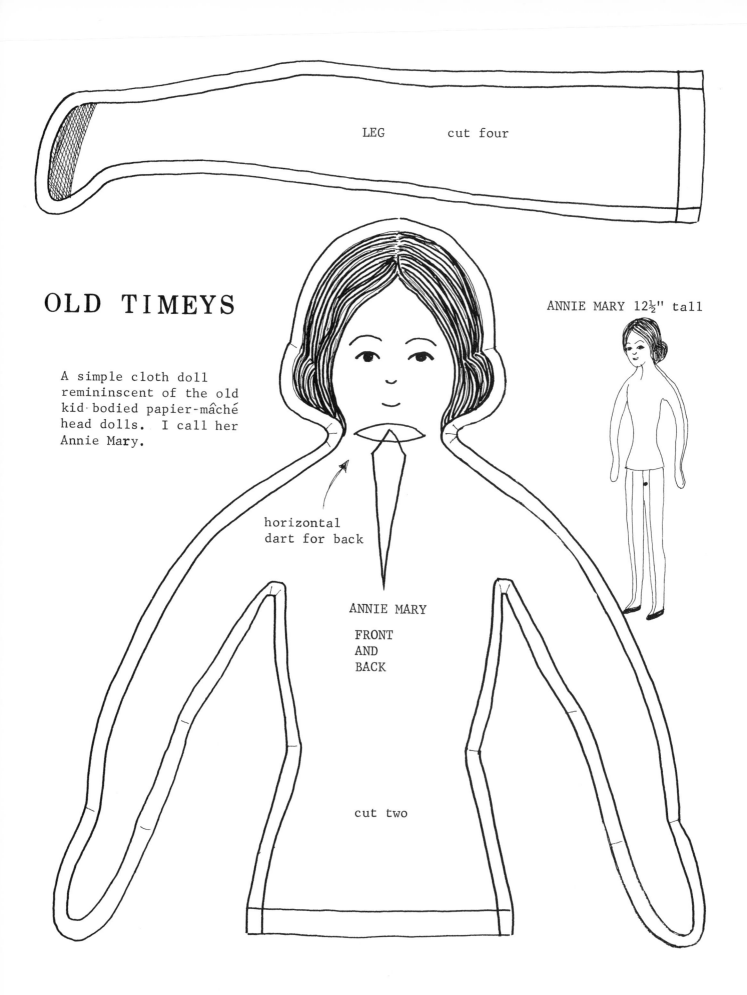

LEG   cut four

OLD TIMEYS

A simple cloth doll
remininscent of the old
kid-bodied papier-mâché
head dolls. I call her
Annie Mary.

ANNIE MARY 12½" tall

horizontal
dart for back

ANNIE MARY

FRONT
AND
BACK

cut two

ANNIE MARY'S CLOTHES

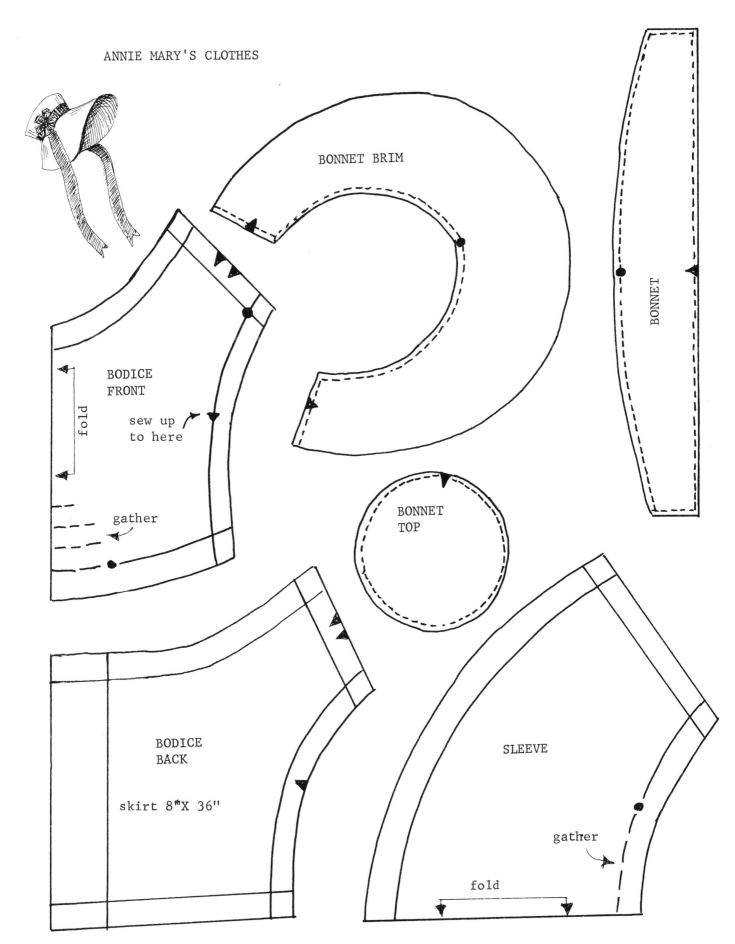

BONNET BRIM

BONNET

BODICE
FRONT

fold

sew up
to here

gather

BONNET
TOP

BODICE
BACK

skirt 8"X 36"

SLEEVE

gather

fold

OLD TIMEYS

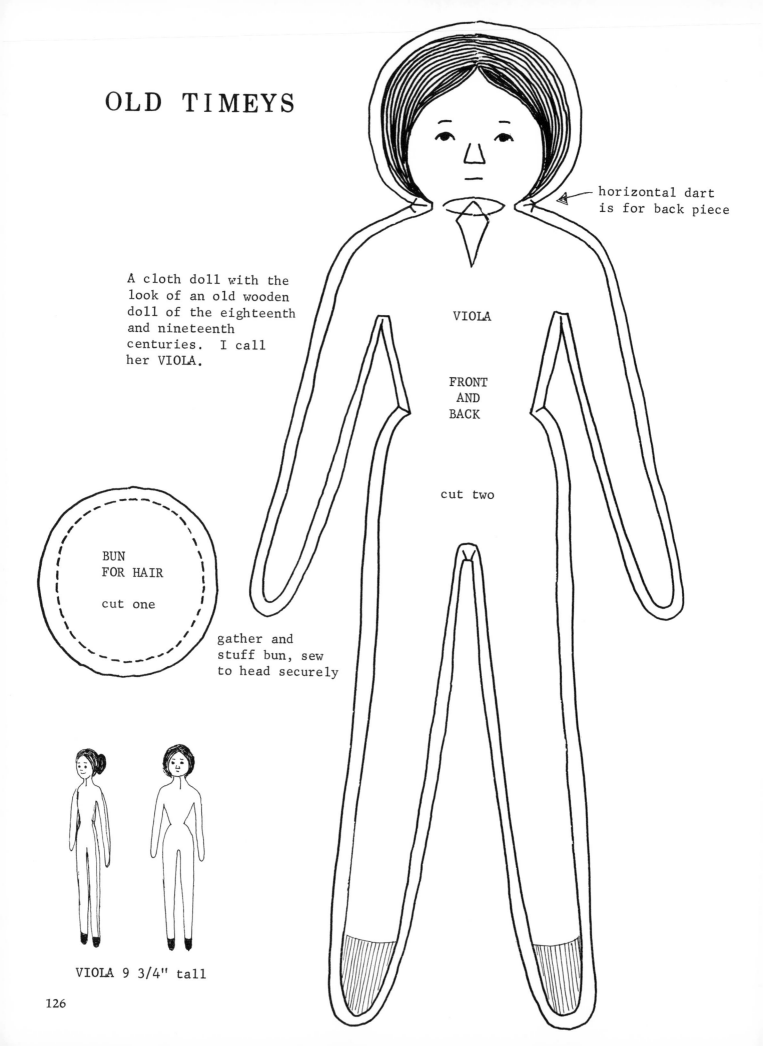

horizontal dart
is for back piece

A cloth doll with the
look of an old wooden
doll of the eighteenth
and nineteenth
centuries. I call
her VIOLA.

VIOLA

FRONT
AND
BACK

cut two

BUN
FOR HAIR

cut one

gather and
stuff bun, sew
to head securely

VIOLA 9 3/4" tall

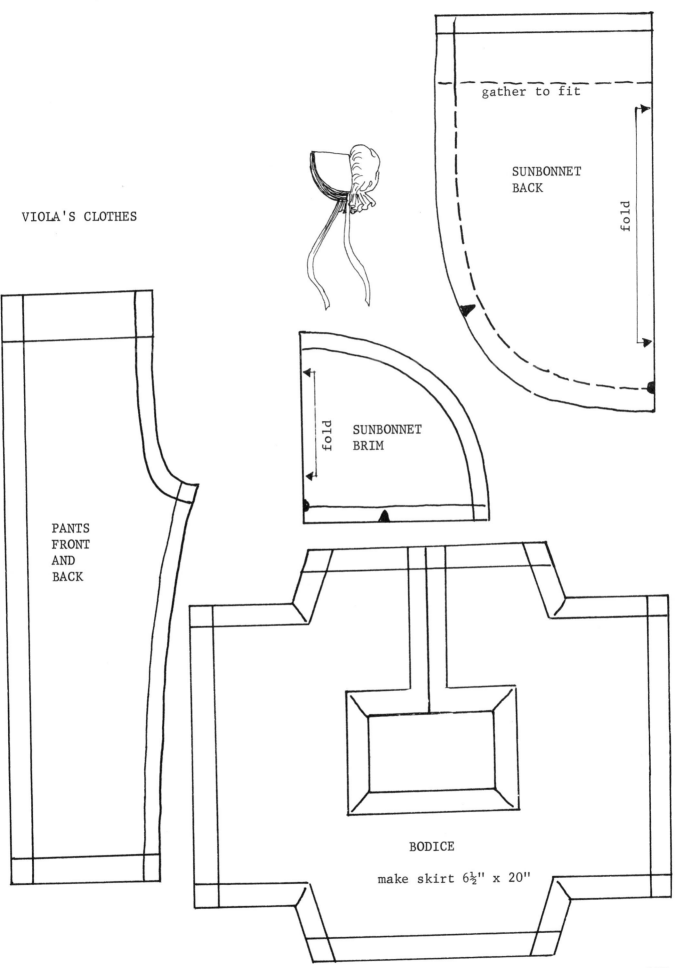

VIOLA'S CLOTHES

gather to fit

SUNBONNET
BACK

fold

SUNBONNET
BRIM

fold

PANTS
FRONT
AND
BACK

BODICE

make skirt 6½" x 20"

127

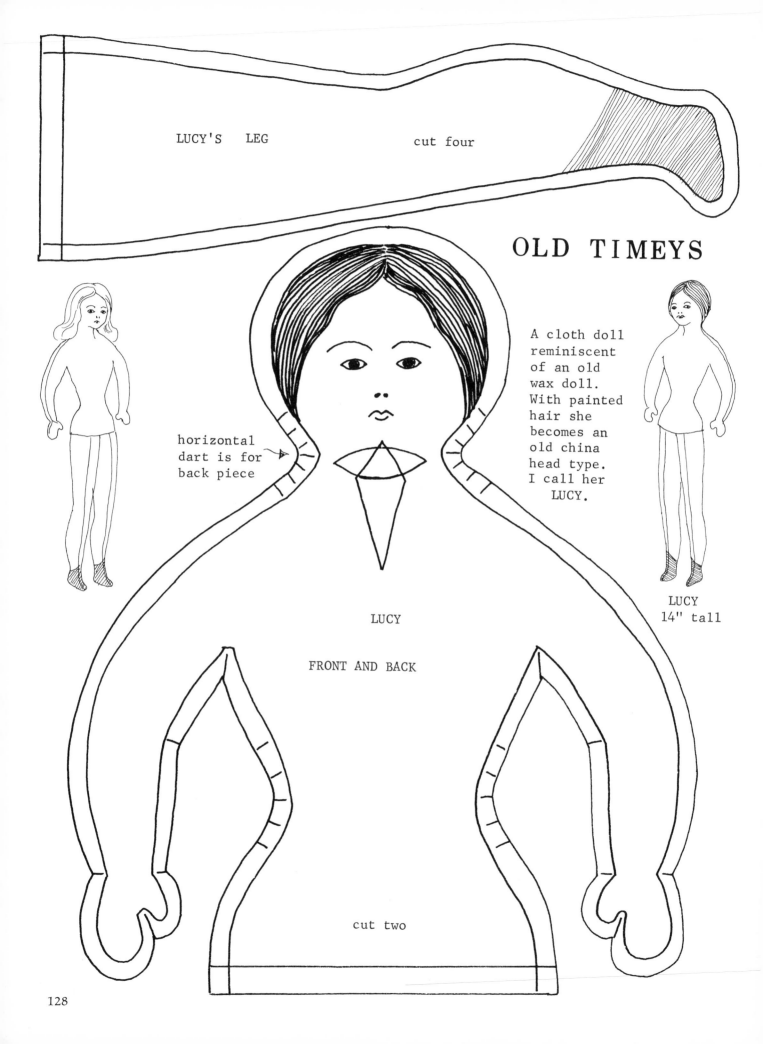

LUCY'S LEG   cut four

OLD TIMEYS

horizontal
dart is for
back piece

A cloth doll
reminiscent
of an old
wax doll.
With painted
hair she
becomes an
old china
head type.
I call her
LUCY.

LUCY

FRONT AND BACK

LUCY
14" tall

cut two

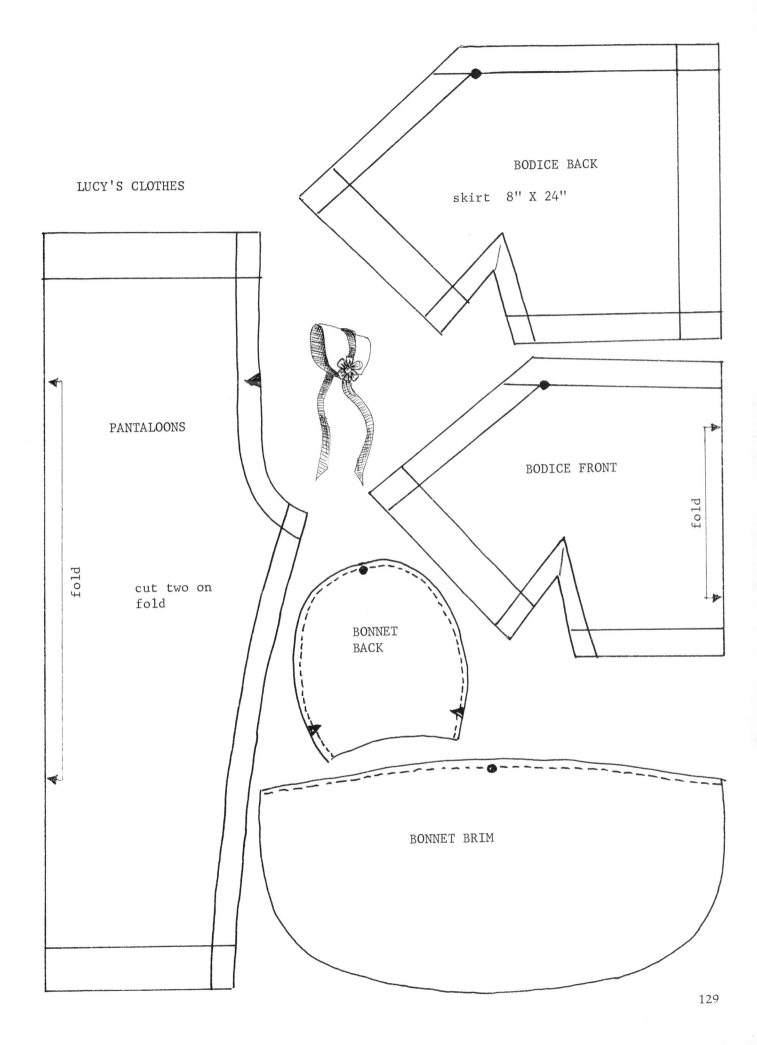

LUCY'S CLOTHES

BODICE BACK

skirt 8" X 24"

PANTALOONS

cut two on
fold

fold

BODICE FRONT

fold

BONNET
BACK

BONNET BRIM

11. Sewing Toys for Young Children

If you plan to give any of these dolls or bears to young children, or if there is a chance that small children may play with them, it is a good idea to check out your plans with the rules set up by the U.S. Consumer Product Safety Commission, Washington, D.C. 20207. Not one of us would ever want to give a child a toy that might hurt him or make him sick. We also would like to believe that, as well as being safe, the toy might be one capable of inspiring creative and intellectual growth.

I have looked at my own creations with a critical eye, considered the Commission's suggestions and rules, and come up with the following list. A few suggestions for preserving the doll and for ideas to stimulate the child's learning are included. Learning should always be an important part of play.

1. Embroider your bear's eyes and nose instead of using buttons.

2. Check all fabrics for dye fastness.

3. Leave off the doll's or bear's eyelashes.

4. Check your cloth, fur fabrics, and hair for fire-resistance.

5. Sew all seams securely so no stuffing comes out.

6. Use only hygenic, new materials instead of recycled ones or those of unknown content.

7. Use no pins for hair bows or fasteners on clothes. Also check your doll carefully to make certain you haven't unintentionally left a pin in the wig or body somewhere during construction.

8. Don't give the hard-face or built-up-nose dolls to young children. Young children often suck on their dolls or bears.

9. If you plan to give the Old Timeys to young children, don't paint them with paint, glue, or wax; just keep them plain cloth. These dolls primarily appeal to older children and adults anyway.

10. Use a nonallergenic stuffing.

11. When using buttons on the doll clothes, be sure to sew them on *securely* and use no metal shank or two-piece buttons.

12. Put an extra layer of cloth or a twill tape inside the doll's arm tabs to prevent the child from tearing the arms off. Young ones often carry a doll or bear by it's arm "Christopher Robin" style.

13. When making the clothes, it will help the young child to be self-sufficient if you open the garments all the way down the back or front so they can be taken on or off with ease.

14. In order to make it easier for the child to learn to manipulate buttons by himself, remember what my mother used to tell me, "The smaller the child, the bigger the button should be."

Index